WHAT A MESS

by Dr. Randy Johnson

with contributions by:
Noble Baird
John Carter
Trevor Cole
Carole Combs
Jayson Combs
Jen Combs
Josh Combs
Jason Duncan
Jeff England
Donna Fox
Barry Harrison
Matt Hatton
Randy Johnson
Scott Johnson
Jill Osmon
Phil Piasecki
Alex Reimen
Josue Rodriguez
John Sanchez
Ryan Story
Kyle Wendel
Ty Woznek
Tommy Youngquist

First Edition, May 2016

Published by:
The River Church
8393 E. Holly Rd.
Holly, MI 48442

Scriptures are taken from the Bible,
English Standard Version (ESV)

Printed in the United States of America

CONTENTS

WEEK 1: CLOSING PANDORA'S BOX

WEEK 2: YOU-NITY

WEEK 3: WIS-DUMB

WEEK 4: PARISH OR PERISH?

WEEK 5: PUFFED OR POWERFUL?

WEEK 6: SATAN'S SERVANT

WEEK 7: TAKE ONE FOR THE TEAM

WEEK 8: THE BED AND BEYOND

WEEK 9: THE SMART OR HEART?

WEEK 10: SPRINT, MARATHON OR OBSTACLE COURSE

WEEK 11: LESSON LEARNED

WEEK 12: THE DEVIL IS IN THE DETAILS

WEEK 13: DEM DRY BONES

WEEK 14: "ALL WE NEED IS..."

WEEK 15: TONGUE TIED

WEEK 16: BACK TO BASICS

WEEK 17: PS: I STILL LOVE YOU

1

CLOSING PANDORA'S BOX

Dr. Randy Johnson | Growth Pastor

In Greek mythology, Zeus gives Pandora a box. She was told not to open the box, but her curiosity won out and she just cracked the lid. All the troubles known to mankind flew out into the world. Today, "Pandora's box" has come to be known as a multitude of sins.

What is the true biblical account of how sin entered the world?

FIRST EVE & THEN ADAM
YIELDED TO THE LIES OF
SATAN GEN 3

On Paul's second missionary journey, he spent time in Corinth (Acts 18:1-17 records Paul's visit to Corinth). He planted a church there. Now, Paul was already on his third missionary journey when he had been given some disturbing news about the lifestyle of the Corinthian believers that needed to be addressed. He wrote 1 Corinthians to address such issues.

Author: Paul

His name went from Saul (inquired of God) to Paul (small or little). How could this be significant?

Recipients: Believers at Corinth

Corinth was the leading commercial center of southern Greece. It was called "the bridge of the sea".

What are the advantages and disadvantages (physically, socially, and spiritually) of being such a visited city?

Key AD dates (approximate):

30 Jesus' Death, Burial, and Resurrection
36 Saul's (Paul) Conversion
47 Paul's Call
48 Paul's 1st Missionary Journey Begins
51 Paul's 2nd Missionary Journey Begins
51 Paul at Corinth
54 Paul's 3rd Missionary Journey Begins
56 Writing of 1 Corinthians
58 Paul's Arrest at Jerusalem
60 Paul's Imprisonment in Rome
64 Paul Goes to Spain

Galatians 1:15-18

But when he who had set me apart before I was born, and who called me by his grace, was pleased to reveal his Son to me, in order that I might preach him among the Gentiles, I did not immediately consult with anyone; nor did I go up to

Jerusalem to those who were apostles before me, but I went away into Arabia, and returned again to Damascus. Then after three years I went up to Jerusalem to visit Cephas and remained with him fifteen days.

What did Saul (Paul) do for three years after his conversion?

WAS TAUGT OF GOD &
WITNESS UNSPEAKALE GLORIES
OF THE THIRD HEAVEN

Acts 13:2 (verse 9 Saul starts being referred to as Paul)
While they were worshiping the Lord and fasting, the Holy Spirit said, "Set apart for me Barnabas and Saul for the work to which I have called them."

Saul (Paul) was saved in about 36 AD, but not called (ordained) until 47. Why do you think this was so?

THAT GOD COULD TAKE HIM
AND TEACH HIM IN PARPARATION
FOR GOD WORK IN HIS LIFE

Chronological Order of Paul's Epistles

Six Epistles before Acts 28:
Galatians (49 or 53-56)
1 Thessalonians (51-52)
2 Thessalonians (51-52)
1 Corinthians (56)
2 Corinthians (56)
Romans (57)

Seven Epistles after Acts 28: (After 60 AD)
Ephesians

Philippians
Philemon
Colossians
1 Timothy
Titus
2 Timothy

(Note: The author of Hebrews is unknown)

1 Corinthians 5:9
I wrote to you in my letter not to associate with sexually immoral people.

This verse is not included in the letters earlier than 1 Corinthians. Could Paul have written a letter that was not inspired by God?
NO! PERHAPS THE PREVIOUS
CHUCHES WERE NOT HAVING
THIS PROBLEM

Theme:
1. Unity
2. Errors of Christian conduct corrected

Remember: The only Bible some people may read is your life.

Key people:
Saul (Paul)
Sosthenes - ruler of the synagogue
Chloe – informs Paul of the sin at Corinth
Cephas - Peter
Crispus and Gaius – baptized by Paul
Stephanas' household - the first converts in Achaia
Aquila and Prisca – tent makers

Apollos – needed further teaching
Acts 18:24
Now a Jew named Apollos, a native of Alexandria, came to Ephesus. He was an eloquent man, competent in the Scriptures.

A complimentary description is given of Apollos. How would you like to be described?

Key topics:
Divisions and unity
Litigation
Sexual Immorality
Marriage
The Lord's Supper
Spiritual Gifts
Love
The Resurrection

Key verses: 1 Corinthians 14:33, 40
For God is not a God of confusion but of peace. As in all the churches of the saints.

But all things should be done decently and in order.

How does this relate to our Gatherings?
THAT WE MEET IN LOVE &
UNDERSTANDING

The Jesus element: 1 Corinthians 1:30
And because of him you are in Christ Jesus, who became to

us wisdom from God, righteousness and sanctification and redemption.

Define the words righteousness, sanctification, and redemption.

TO COMPLETLY FOLLOW GOD'S WAY

TO BE SET APART FOR A GIVEN PLAN

TO BE COMPLITLY CLENSED OF SIN!

Whose work made it possible for me to be saved (redemption)?

JESUS TOOK ALL FOR ME!

PEOPLE WHO PRAYED FOR MY WALKING IN BLIND [illegible]

Whose work makes it possible for me to grow in my walk (righteousness and sanctification)?

MY LORD AND SAVIOR JESUS CHRIST!!!

Familiar verses in 1 Corinthians:

1:18 - ***For the word of the cross is folly to those who are perishing, but to us who are being saved it is the power of God.***

2:9 - ***But, as it is written, "What no eye has seen, nor ear heard, nor the heart of man imagined, what God has prepared for those who love him"***

6:19-20 - ***Or do you not know that your body is a temple of the Holy Spirit within you, whom you have from God? You are not your own, for you were bought with a price. So glorify God in your body.***

9:24 - ***Do you not know that in a race all the runners run, but only one receives the prize? So run that you may obtain it.***

10:13 - ***No temptation has overtaken you that is not common to man. God is faithful, and he will not let you be tempted beyond your ability, but with the temptation he will also provide the way of escape, that you may be able to endure it.***

10:31 - ***So, whether you eat or drink, or whatever you do, do all to the glory of God.***

11:26 - ***For as often as you eat this bread and drink the cup, you proclaim the Lord's death until he comes.***

12:12 - ***For just as the body is one and has many members, and all the members of the body, though many, are one body, so it is with Christ.***

13:4-8a - ***Love is patient and kind; love does not envy or boast; it is not arrogant or rude. It does not insist on its own way; it is not irritable or resentful; it does not rejoice at wrongdoing, but rejoices with the truth. Love bears all things, believes all things, hopes all things, endures all things.***
Love never ends.

13:13 - ***So now faith, hope, and love abide, these three; but the greatest of these is love.***

Which of these verses is your favorite? Why?
I HAVE NO FAVORITE — I LOVE
GOD'S WORD!!

PANDORA'S BOX

Dr. Randy Johnson | Growth Pastor

In Greek mythology, Zeus gives Pandora a box. She was told not to open the box, but her curiosity won out, and she just cracked the lid. All the troubles known to mankind flew out into the world. Today, "Pandora's box" has come to be known as a multitude of sins.

Somehow, every worldview has to account for how sin entered the world. The Bible starts with creation and immediately shows how sin entered the world (Genesis 3). Sin entered the world by the disobedience of Adam and Eve. 1 Corinthians 15:21 gives a strong contrast between Adam and Jesus,
"For as by a man came death, by a man has come also the resurrection of the dead." Adam's sin brought death. Jesus' death covered man's sin and allowed for life again, life eternal.

As we study 1 Corinthians, we are going to see them regularly struggle with sin. Paul takes the time to write a lengthy letter pointing out their sin. He does not write as an arrogant judge, but as a friend and mentor who wants the best for them. Their moral problems have created divisions in the church. Paul tries to bring unity.

Jeremiah 17:9 says, ***"The heart is deceitful above all things, and desperately sick; who can understand it?" We, like the Corinthians, will struggle with sin. Hopefully, we have a friend and mentor who will be willing to point out our steps before destruction leaves deep scars.***

We are reminded at the Lord's Supper to examine ourselves

regularly. Personally, I appreciate David's words and heart in Psalm 139:23-24:

"Search me, O God, and know my heart!
Try me and know my thoughts!
And see if there be any grievous way in me,
and lead me in the way everlasting!"

Hopefully, our study in 1 Corinthians will not simply be a spectator mindset noticing how bad they were. As we study Scripture, we need to invite the Lord to do a little house cleaning in our heart and mind.

"Give me one hundred preachers who fear nothing but sin and desire nothing but God, and I care not whether they be clergymen or laymen, they alone will shake the gates of Hell and set up the kingdom of Heaven upon Earth." John Wesley

TOGETHER WE CAN

Dr. Randy Johnson | Growth Pastor

Amongst the sin and selfishness, Paul in 1 Corinthians says a lot about unity. Unity is vitally important, and the danger of all these sins is they tend to divide us. Colossians 3:13-14 says, "Bear with each other and forgive one another if any of you has a grievance against someone. Forgive as the Lord forgave you. And over all these virtues put on love, which binds them all together in perfect unity." There are several roads to unity. Forgiveness and love tend to be the ones most often used and needed.

Ravi Zacharias has said, "Where destruction is the motive, unity is dangerous. For example, if I have evil intent and I galvanize that evil intent with many others, the capacity to destroy is immense. Where goodness is the motive, unity is phenomenal and actually has some good issues to it." Perfect unity is working together for the cause of Christ. It is something bigger than we are. Romans 12:16 says, ***"Live in harmony with one another. Do not be haughty, but associate with the lowly. Never be wise in your own sight." Unity takes work.***

There is power in unity. Ignatius of Antioch said, "Take heed, then, often to come together to give thanks to God, and show forth His praise. For when you assemble frequently in the same place, the powers of Satan are destroyed, and the destruction at which he aims is prevented by the unity of your faith."

The story that has challenged me the most on unity is that of Jonathan and David. Jonathan could have felt entitled to be the next king. He could have listened to the many voices urging him there. He could have sided with his dad. However, 1 Samuel 23:16

says, ***"And Jonathan, Saul's son, rose and went to David at Horesh, and strengthened his hand in God."*** Jonathan was more concerned on what God wanted than what he "deserved." He chose unity.

Remember: They will know we are Christians by our love.

Has God placed someone on your mind? Seek unity.

"Behold, how good and pleasant it is
   when brothers dwell in unity!" - Psalm 133:1

SWEET FRIENDSHIP

Dr. Randy Johnson | Growth Pastor

The basic themes of 1 Corinthians are:
1. Unity
2. Errors of Christian conduct corrected

As I spent time in the book, I became more and more challenged with the concept of these two themes coming together. To have unity, we must be willing to point out the moral discrepancies in other believers. I am not promoting the bashing of unbelievers. I expect an unbeliever to live consistently within their worldview. It is the erring believer that we need to approach in love.

Proverbs 27:17 says, ***"Iron sharpens iron, and one man sharpens another."*** When this is done regularly, we do not have to have as big of a clash. While in college, I worked in a factory over the summer and any other break. It was the coveted 5:00 pm to 4:30 am shift. My job was to smooth out the edges of metal pieces using a grinding wheel. Smaller "snags" typically came off easy. However, if a piece burned too long during the cutting stage, it could destroy a piece. We need to sharpen each other. This can be done by exposing sin, weaknesses, or even by complimenting accomplishments and strengths. Balance is good.

I am not sure you can have perfect unity if errors of Christian conduct are not corrected. Sin going unaddressed is not unity. Unity comes from thinking and walking together in the mind of Christ.

Gatherings are important so we can, ***"consider how to stir up one another to love and good works"*** (Hebrews 10:24). Teamwork does not get overemphasized. Great teams have unity.

Proverbs 27:9 says, ***"Oil and perfume make the heart glad, and the sweetness of a friend comes from his earnest counsel."*** That is such a beautiful picture and analogy. Unity comes from a friend's counsel. It might not be what we want to hear, but it is still compared to perfume and sweetness.

"There is nothing on this earth more to be prized than true friendship." Thomas Aquinas

"I cannot even imagine where I would be today were it not for that handful of friends who have given me a heart full of joy. Let's face it, friends make life a lot more fun." Charles R. Swindoll

Take time today to thank a friend.

Take time today to be a friend.

"My best friend is the one who brings out the best in me." Henry Ford

REPUTATION

Dr. Randy Johnson | Growth Pastor

Some years ago, I was out for a run when I ran into my high school history teacher. I had not seen him in about 25 years. He had not changed. I viewed most my teachers as "old," and now he was. He taught at Warren Fitzgerald his whole teaching career. We had talked some while I was in school, but I knew he had thousands of thousands of students come through his class. I introduced myself, and he said, "Johnson, baseball player and a Baptist." Obviously, I wish he had said a Christian (and a great baseball player). As I thought about it, I was pleased on how he remembered me.

Several people are listed in 1 Corinthians. There is Saul (Paul), Sosthenes
Chloe, Cephas (Peter), Crispus, Gaius, Stephanas, Aquila, Prisca, and a leader by the name of Apollos. Not much is known of Apollos. However, Acts 18:24 says, ***"Now a Jew named Apollos, a native of Alexandria, came to Ephesus. He was an eloquent man, competent in the Scriptures."***

A complimentary description is given of Apollos. He was eloquent and competent. He knew the Word. That is such a great reputation to have. Benjamin Franklin warned, "It takes many good deeds to build a good reputation, and only one bad one to lose it." We need to focus on character and hope the truth will be seen and heard through reputation. Dwight L. Moody said it this way, "If I take care of my character, my reputation will take care of me."

Proverbs 22:1 says, ***"A good name is to be chosen rather than great riches, and favor is better than silver or gold."*** Having a good name is a priority.

George Washington said, “Associate with men of good quality if you esteem your own reputation; for it is better to be alone than in bad company.” We all know the phrase “guilty by association.” Could we be guilty of good things through association? I think so.

Finally, Acts 24:16 says, ***“So I always take pains to have a clear conscience toward both God and man.”***

What are you known for?
What do you want to be known for?
What are you going to do about it?

The way to gain a good reputation is to endeavor to be what you desire to appear. Socrates

ORDERLY

Dr. Randy Johnson | Growth Pastor

I am organized; my wife is clean. It is an oversimplification, but it does summarize us well. I will "straighten up" the kitchen after a meal, and then she will come through with the bleach. I like to put things where they are supposed to be. Early in our marriage, if my wife wanted to get my attention, she would "move" something on my desk. Simply stated, she got my attention. I need to be careful how I esteem the value of orderliness, but it is important.

The great philosopher (or, at least, fun cooking show host) Paula Deen has said, "I am guilty of buying way too many gadgets - way too many! And though I try to keep things nice and orderly, sometimes I get distracted and stick saucepans where the stockpots should go." Most people can relate. We get frustrated when we cannot find things because they are not where they are supposed to be. Even in her freelance way, she has a sense of order with her recipes (plus a pound of butter). We like a sense of order.

Most writers choose 1 Corinthians 14:33 and 40 as the key verses for 1 Corinthians: ***"For God is not a God of confusion but of peace. As in all the churches of the saints. But all things should be done decently and in order."*** God is a God of order. Order does bring peace. Confusion happens when we are rattled, frazzled, and out of control.

Orderliness is when people take pride in themselves and what is around them. They take the time to become aware of everything that is going on in their lives that they choose to handle in a certain order.

WEEK 1

In Job 25:2, it says, ***"Dominion and awe belong to God; he establishes order in the heights of heaven."*** If we are made in God's image, I think there is some part of us that can be orderly.

This week appreciate the purposely-planned order of worship.

"To love rightly is to love what is orderly and beautiful in an educated and disciplined way." - Plato

BIBLE VERSE BUFFET

Dr. Randy Johnson | Growth Pastor

As we get ready to jump into a chapter-a-week, verse-by-verse look at the Book of 1 Corinthians, I thought I would whet your appetite with some of the familiar verses in 1 Corinthians:

1:18 - ***For the word of the cross is folly to those who are perishing, but to us who are being saved it is the power of God.***

2:9 - ***But, as it is written, "What no eye has seen, nor ear heard, nor the heart of man imagined, what God has prepared for those who love him"***

6:19-20 - ***Or do you not know that your body is a temple of the Holy Spirit within you, whom you have from God? You are not your own, for you were bought with a price. So glorify God in your body.***

9:24 - ***Do you not know that in a race all the runners run, but only one receives the prize? So run that you may obtain it.***

10:13 - ***No temptation has overtaken you that is not common to man. God is faithful, and he will not let you be tempted beyond your ability, but with the temptation he will also provide the way of escape, that you may be able to endure it.***

10:31 - ***So, whether you eat or drink, or whatever you do, do all to the glory of God.***

11:26 - ***For as often as you eat this bread and drink the cup, you proclaim the Lord's death until he comes.***

12:12 - ***For just as the body is one and has many members, and all the members of the body, though many, are one body, so it is with Christ.***

13:4-8a - ***Love is patient and kind; love does not envy or boast; it is not arrogant or rude. It does not insist on its own way; it is not irritable or resentful; it does not rejoice at wrongdoing, but rejoices with the truth. Love bears all things, believes all things, hopes all things, endures all things. Love never ends.***

13:13 - ***So now faith, hope, and love abide, these three; but the greatest of these is love.***

Did one verse catch your attention more than the others did?

Write out the verse. Take it with you. Memorize it. Meditate on it.

Please pray that the next 16 weeks will be fruitful as you and the church study the Book of 1 Corinthians.

WEEK 1

2

YOU-NITY

Dr. Randy Johnson | Growth Pastor

Paul gives a typical welcome, but quickly starts to address the topic of divisions. You can be the key to unity.

Who was your closest friend growing up? What adventures did you dream up? ______________________________

____

____

Who were Paul's closest friends? ______________________________

____

____

1 Paul, called by the will of God to be an apostle of Christ Jesus, and our brother Sosthenes,

Acts 18:17

And they all seized Sosthenes, the ruler of the synagogue, and beat him in front of the tribunal. But Gallio paid no attention to any of this.

Who is Sosthenes and why did he get beaten but not Paul?

____

Would this have brought him and Paul closer together?

2 To the church of God that is in Corinth, to those sanctified in Christ Jesus, called to be saints together with all those who in every place call upon the name of our Lord Jesus Christ, both their Lord and ours:

Is he writing to a pagan or Christian audience?

Sanctified means "set apart for God". Saints means "set apart ones". Knowing the topics he will cover in this book, why do you think he uses these words with his readers?

"Has it ever occurred to you that one hundred pianos all tuned to the same fork are automatically tuned to each other? They are of one accord by being tuned, not to each other, but to another standard to which each one must individually bow. So one hundred worshipers met together, each one looking away to Christ, are in heart nearer to each other than they could possibly be, were they to become 'unity' conscious and turn their eyes away from God to strive for closer fellowship." A.W. Tozer

3 Grace to you and peace from God our Father and the Lord Jesus Christ.4 I give thanks to my God always for you because of the grace of God that was given you in Christ Jesus, 5 that in every way you were enriched in him in all speech and all knowledge— 6 even as the testimony about Christ was confirmed among you— 7 so that you are not lacking in any gift, as you wait for the revealing of our Lord Jesus Christ, 8 who will sustain you to the end, guiltless in the day of our Lord Jesus Christ. 9 God is faithful, by whom you were called into the fellowship of his Son, Jesus Christ our Lord.

Knowing all the sin Paul will address in this letter, why do you think he starts with giving thanks for them? ________________

THEY STARTED RIGHT

BUT NEED TO GET BACK ON TRACK

What truths about God does Paul affirm in these verses?

HE HAS GUIDED THEM

BUT THEY NEED TO EXAMINE

THEMSELVES & GET BACK

Romans 8:33 says, ***"Who shall bring any charge against God's elect? It is God who justifies."*** How does this verse relate to verse 8?

10 I appeal to you, brothers, by the name of our Lord Jesus Christ, that all of you agree, and that there be no divisions among you, but that you be united in the same mind and the same judgment. 11 For it has been reported to me by Chloe's people that there is quarreling among you, my brothers. 12 What I mean is that each one of you says, "I follow Paul," or "I follow Apollos," or "I follow Cephas," or "I follow Christ."

13 Is Christ divided? Was Paul crucified for you? Or were you baptized in the name of Paul? 14 I thank God that I baptized none of you except Crispus and Gaius, 15 so that no one may say that you were baptized in my name. 16 (I did baptize also the household of Stephanas. Beyond that, I do not know whether I baptized anyone else.) 17 For Christ did not send me to baptize but to preach the gospel, and not with words of eloquent wisdom, lest the cross of Christ be emptied of its power.

What divisions are reported here?

When this letter was first read out loud, Paul may have fed their strife by referring to himself, Apollos, and Cephas (verse 12) only to deflate their arguments when he mentions following Christ (Is there possibly some sarcasm here?).

Should a focus on verse 17 settle most divisions in the church?

Visual thinkers, how do you picture the cross of Christ be emptied of its power (verse 17)?

"Love was compressed for all history in that lonely figure on the cross, who said that he could call down angels at any moment on a rescue mission, but chose not to – because of us. At Calvary, God accepted his own unbreakable terms of justice." Philip Yancey

18 For the word of the cross is folly to those who are perishing, but to us who are being saved it is the power of God. 19 For it is written, "I will destroy the wisdom of the wise, and the discernment of the discerning I will thwart." 20 Where is the one who is wise? Where is the scribe? Where is the debater of this age? Has not God made foolish the wisdom of the world? 21 For since, in the wisdom of God, the world did not know God through wisdom, it pleased God through the folly of what we preach to save those who believe. 22 For Jews demand signs and Greeks seek wisdom, 23 but we preach Christ crucified, a stumbling block to Jews and folly to Gentiles, 24 but to those who are called, both Jews and Greeks, Christ the power of God and the wisdom of God. 25 For the foolishness of God is wiser than men, and the weakness of God is stronger than men.

What is the word (message) of the cross (verse 18)?

GOD IS ALL — NOT MAN

What messages of the world differ from God's teaching?

THEIR SO-CALLED WISDOM. ETC IS NOT GOD'S

How is preaching Christ crucified a stumbling block to Jews and folly to Gentiles (verse 23)? THEY LOOK TO EVERYTHING BUT THE WAY THAT CHIST SHOWS

26 For consider your calling, brothers: not many of you were wise according to worldly standards, not many were powerful, not many were of noble birth. 27 But God chose what is foolish in the world to shame the wise; God chose what is weak in the world to shame the strong; 28 God chose what is low and despised in the world, even things that are not, to bring to nothing things that are, 29 so that no human being might boast in the presence of God. 30 And because of him you are in Christ Jesus, who became to us wisdom from God, righteousness and sanctification and redemption, 31 so that, as it is written, "Let the one who boasts, boast in the Lord."

Give examples from Scripture where God used the unexpected to do the unimaginable? ______

RAISE THE DEAD & UNTOLD MIRACLES

Who and what you are is a gift from God, so in what ways can we boast in the Lord? ______

ONLY IN CHRIST JESUS

Who has been a hero for you in your Christian walk?

MANY CHURCH BROTHERS & SISTERS

What from his or her life do you want to build in your own?

A WILLINGNESS TO FOLLOW HIS WILL FOR MY LIFE

"God did not direct His call to Isaiah— Isaiah overheard God saying, ". . . who will go for Us?" The call of God is not just for a select few but for everyone. Whether I hear God's call or not depends on the condition of my ears, and exactly what I hear depends upon my spiritual attitude." Oswald Chambers

1 CORINTHIANS 1: DEVOTION 1

NEW TO THE BIBLE

Jen Combs | Wife of Lead Pastor Josh Combs

This summer as a church, we are going to be traveling through the book of 1 Corinthians. I remember the very first time I ever studied this book. I was 18 years old sitting in my mother-in-law's (well, she wasn't quite my mother-in-law yet) Sunday school class at Faith Church. I was a newer believer and to be honest, didn't know much about the Bible. It is quite an intimidating compilation of books. Sure, I knew stories, even memorized verses in AWANA, but I had no idea how to study or really read the Word. In that class, I learned something that helped me understand a lot of the New Testament. From Acts to Revelation they are all letters. They are letters written to a specific place and specific people. That was such a huge light bulb moment in my life. It may sound silly, but check it out for yourself. Crack open God's Word and look. They all start out with a greeting telling who is writing, then the large part, the body, and then finally, they end with a closing. Pretty cool, huh?

So before I begin reading any book of the Bible I research a few things.

1. Who wrote it?
2. Who they are writing it to?
3. Why they wrote it?
4. Lastly, I pray God gives me understanding.

Without the Holy Spirit revealing the meaning of His Word to me, I am up a creek without a paddle. I need His wisdom to understand. (1 Corinthians 2:10, ***"these things God has revealed to us through the Spirit"***)

Sometimes I just flip to the back of my Bible where it gives a little commentary on the specific book. It helps me get a grasp on just what in the world I am trying to read. Sometimes that means I hit up Google (which you do have to be careful about, not every person out there is biblically sound). Other times it means I just simply ask someone smarter than me. With all of that said, let's dig in...

The apostle Paul wrote 1 Corinthians. Do you remember reading about a man named Saul in the New Testament? Saul was the guy who killed and persecuted Christians. He actually hunted them down! Saul stood by as a great man named Stephen was stoned to death. However, Saul was a smart man who was top of his Jewish class and was a Roman citizen (Those were both fancy things to be during Saul's time). Seriously, read Acts 22:3-21, it is one of the coolest stories to read. You could also go to Acts 9. God radically saves this man Saul and changes his name to Paul. He becomes one of the most influential men for Christ. I tell you all of this, so you have a little understanding of the man who is writing this letter.

Paul is writing to the church in a city called Corinth. Corinth was a huge trade city. They had a terrible reputation for sexual immorality, religious diversity, and corruption. One commentary I read said that even to the Pagan world this city was known for its moral corruption. Sounds like a great place to start a church to me! Paul did just that, he planted a church in the middle of all this chaos. As you can probably assume, the church buckled under all of the worldly pressures. One of the areas the Corinthians really struggled with was unity. They stunk at it. They had division over everything, spiritual gifts, marriage, idols, and even the resurrection. Pauls' letter is meant to help set them straight in all of these areas.

I hope you make it a priority to stick with us from the beginning to the end of this study. I pray for myself and all of you that God will reveal His spiritual truth as we study together the book of 1 Corinthians.

SET APART

Jen Combs | Wife of Lead Pastor Josh Combs

Today Paul is writing to believers in the city of Corinth. Verse 2 says, ***"To the church of God that is in Corinth, to those sanctified in Christ Jesus."***

Sanctified is a fancy word for being set apart or holy. It is the process that God has us go through here on earth. I have given Jesus my life, and until I die, I will continue to be sanctified. Continuing to grow and be more like Christ every day. He is constantly molding me and shaping me.

I think it is important to understand that this is written to believers. His words of instruction and correction are to believers, to those who bear the name of brother or sister, fellow followers of Jesus. So often, I get frustrated with the unbelievers in my life because they do not behave as believers do or should. They do not have the same priorities. Then I read something like this and go..."ugh some days Combs, you are such an idiot." (Sorry, letting some of my inner dialogue out there.) It is a reminder for me to worry about me. I am a believer in Christ... me, Jen Combs. I have enough to work on. I should not be concerned with the unbeliever's behavior. I will keep working on me and be a light for Jesus to them. If I am hollering or getting annoyed for decisions they make or words they say, that does not help. You can win people for Christ by your conduct. They are watching, so be a light in their darkness.

Continuing in verse 2 it says, ***"called to be saints together with all those who IN EVERY PLACE CALL UPON THE NAME OF THE LORD JESUS CHRIST."*** As always, God's Word is alive, active, and sharper than any two-edged sword. I read that part,

and it gripped my heart. Sure, I am a believer, a follower of Christ, but do I "In every place call on his name?" Ouch, that one hurt. Do you or I call on His name when at the grocery store? Do I represent Him when I am out getting a haircut? How about when I am stuck in traffic or having a "discussion" with my spouse? In every place? How about your workplace? Grabbing a coffee? Family gatherings? What about when we are out to eat? IN EVERY PLACE CALL ON HIS NAME. What does that mean exactly? I think it means not being embarrassed by Him. For example, pray when you are out in public. I remember when Josh and I first started dating, and I was out with his family having a meal. Before our food came, we all bowed our heads, and someone started praying. I vividly remember thinking, "Everyone is going to be staring at us, hurry up with that prayer!" I did not grow up praying when we were out in public. Now I realize what a great testimony that is a way to be a light to those around you. Has there ever been a time in your life when you have been talking to someone and you know you could bring the conversation to Jesus and don't? I know I have. You get nervous and worry you will not have the right words. I remember having a garage sale, and the Lord told me to pray with a woman I was talking to, I chickened out and disobeyed. I repented, Jesus forgave me, and you can bet your buttons the next opportunity God gave me, I did not miss it. IN EVERY PLACE, CALL ON HIS NAME. Use those opportunities He gives you to proclaim His name. So, I challenge you this week. IN EVERY PLACE, CALL ON HIS NAME. I want to hear about them. Email me your story of God giving you an opportunity to call on his name this week.
JenCombs@theriverchurch.cc

ELOQUENT WORDS

Jen Combs | Wife of Lead Pastor Josh Combs

"For Christ did not send me to baptize, but to preach the gospel and not with words of eloquent wisdom, lest the cross of Christ be emptied of its power." (1 Corinthians 1:17)

When I heard we were going to be studying 1 Corinthians and was asked to put together a few devotions. I immediately knew I wanted this chapter, solely based on this verse. It is one of my favorites; I find so much comfort in the words, ***"not with eloquent wisdom."*** See, if you had told me 15 years ago that God was going to use me to pray with ladies, teach Bible studies, train volunteers, teach parenting and marriage classes, I would have laughed in your face. I do not speak with eloquent words. I do not know enough about the Bible. I could not possibly do any of those things. Do you notice what the first word is in the last three sentences? "I." Read the rest of that verse, ***"Lest the cross of Christ be emptied of its power."*** Only with Jesus are any of those things possible. It is only through His power. I often pray for wisdom because I do not have the words to comfort people when they are hurting. I do not have eloquent words to use in teaching. However, Jesus does, and I pray daily that He will use me. Last August when we traveled down to the women's prison in Ohio, I was so nervous for days knowing we were going to have the opportunity to pray with these ladies. Would I say what they needed to hear? What if I completely botch it? What if I completely go blank? What if I don't talk loud enough? So I started praying, "Lord use me and give me the right words." Praying that prayer repeatedly for days, God showed up in a real way. I am still amazed at what God did in that prison yard. It was as if I could not stop praying, it felt like the words were just flowing out of my mouth. It was a complete miracle of God.

He heard my prayer and answered. The ladies were so receptive. I learned that God did not need me to have eloquent words but just be willing, and He would take care of the rest. Just like Moses in the Old Testament Exodus 4: 10 records, ***"But Moses said to the Lord, 'Oh my Lord, I am not eloquent, either in the past or since you have spoken to your servant, but I am slow of speech and of tongue.' Then the Lord said to him, 'Who has made mans mouth? Who makes him mute, or deaf, or seeing or blind? Is it not I, the Lord? Now therefore go, and I will be with your mouth and teach you what you shall speak.'"***

Have you ever used all of those excuses before? Throw them out the door and start praying for God to use you and give you the right words, for whatever situation. Be willing, and He will use your mouth and teach you what to speak.

1 CORINTHIANS 1: DEVOTION 4

"FOR THE BIBLE TELLS ME SO"

Jen Combs | Wife of Lead Pastor Josh Combs

1 Corinthians 1:18 says, ***"For the Word of the cross is folly to those who are perishing, but to us who are being saved it is the power of God."*** The Word of God is folly to those who are not believers (those perishing). The Word of God is silly, stupid, and ridiculous to unbelievers. It makes no sense. It holds no weight in their lives; it is meaningless. When I looked up the definition for folly, it said madness and lunacy. Ever have someone who does not believe in Christ look at you as if you have gone mad? Well, apparently that is biblical. Read the second half of that verse... ***"but to us who are being saved it is the power of God."*** To us who are being saved, the Word of God is everything. At least is should be.

Does the Word of God hold that much weight in your life?
Is it your final authority?
Does it get the last say when you are stating your beliefs?

Sometimes when I talk to believers, they will tell me that they follow Christ but then have some crazy idea of say what marriage looks like. They will tell me what their belief on drinking is, how they feel about suffering, and what they think about blessing. In my Bible, I have a statement I heard once written down, "Am I defending a position or seeking the truth of God's Word." Is how I think a family should operate based on my feelings and how I think it should operate? Do I look at God's Word and say, "Ok God, teach me what a family should look like." God's Word is my filter for everything (or, at least, I try to make it that way). What I think about drinking, what I think about divorce, what I think about money, and parenting, I run it through the filter of His Word. What does the Bible say about that? Even doctrine. Some people are tangled up in poor doctrine, and they believe it just because their grandma taught it to them or a pastor years ago said it was so. What does God's Word say on the matter?

Here is a hot topic for you, what does the Bible say I should think about government? Paying taxes? What does the Bible say about how the earth was created? How to handle a disagreement? What does the Bible say about aliens? I am talking EVERYTHING here folks! The Bible should be your filter for everything. Make sure your opinion mirrors what God's Word says.

WHAT IS YOUR CALLING?

Jen Combs | Wife of Lead Pastor Josh Combs

1 Corinthians 1:26-29, ***"For consider your calling, brothers: not many of you were wise according to worldly standards, not many were powerful, not many were born of noble birth. But God chose what is foolish in the world to shame the wise; God chose what is weak in the world to shame the strong; God chose what is low and despised in the world, even things that are not, to bring to nothing things that are, so that no human being might boast in the presence of God."***

Consider your calling. What do you do for a living? Are you a teacher, plumber, police officer, nurse, stay at home mom, in sales, a banker, or whatever your calling? Consider it; Scripture says that most of us are not super wise according to the world standards, we are not super powerful on a worldwide scale, and I do not think I know anyone of noble birth. However, God chose you; He chose the unexpected. He chose the unlikely candidate. He chose the underdog. He chose you to be His ambassador on Earth. I do not know about you, but in a world that chews you up and spits you out so often, I find extreme comfort in knowing that I am chosen by the King. However, what am I chosen for?

2 Corinthians 5:19-20 says, ***"...entrusting to us the message of reconciliation. Therefore, we are ambassadors of Christ."*** The actual definition of an ambassador is an accredited diplomat sent by a country as its official representative to a foreign country. God chose you to be His official representative to this lost world. Once you gave your life to Christ, you became a citizen of heaven, no longer a citizen of this world. You are His ambassador to this foreign country. You are sent by Him as a representative of His to

the lost to share His message of reconciliation, which is just a big word for salvation. When was the last time you shared the Gospel with anyone? Are you serving in a ministry to help the Gospel go forward? Matthew 28 talks about how we are to make disciples, teach them the Word. Are you discipling anyone? Trust me you do not have to know it all to teach someone. You do not have to have eloquent words. You do not even have to be sure of yourself, just be sure of the Bible. Trust that God will give you the words and you just simply teach them what you know. Even if that is not a lot, keep learning and keep teaching. If you do not have anyone to disciple and are ready for that, we will happily connect you with someone. So please do not hesitate to ask.

THERE IS A "YOU" IN UNITY

Jen Combs | Wife of Lead Pastor Josh Combs

I really have struggled with writing this devotion. Unity. God calls us to be united in this cause for Christ. It seems simple enough. I wanted to write...unity, just do it. How hard is it to be united with everyone who claims to be a Christ follower?

1 Corinthians 1:10 says, ***"I appeal to you brothers, by the name of our Lord Jesus Christ, that all of you agree and that there be no divisions among you, but that you be united in the same mind and in the same judgment. For it has been reported to me by Chloe's people that there is quarreling among you, my brothers."***

Have you ever met a bunch of people who love to disagree as much as the church body? Sheesh, you have people leave churches because of paint colors, they do not like the music, they do not like the children's program, it is too big, it is too small, the Pastor does not preach exactly how they like, some want pews, some want chairs, blah blah blah. You name it, and I have probably heard the excuses to why people argue or leave a church. We do not like this one, so we are just going to leave and start another one. How ungodly is that? God does not receive glory in our quarreling or separating. For the greater good of the Gospel, we need to lay preferences and hurt down.

What does God call us to be united over? His doctrine. God puts into place Pastoral leadership in our local church bodies. These men are called by God and held responsible for teach us God's Word. Hebrews 13:17 says, ***"Obey your leaders and submit to them, for they are keeping watch over your souls, as those who will have to give an account."*** As long as a Pastor is preaching

God's Word faithfully and is living their lives in accordance with the qualifications of a pastor in 1 Timothy, we have got to put the rest aside and be united in the Scripture. We may not prefer the methods they use or like decisions they have made. However, if they do not go against Scripture, we are to remain unified.

Over the last few months, The River Church and The Point Church unified. This was not an easy decision to make. What if they do not do things how we do them, what if they spend money differently than we do, what if I do not get to make decisions how I want them, what if they run their programs differently, what if, what if, what if. However, all of the pastors involved in making this decision put aside their preferences in order for us to collectively reach and minister to more people with the Gospel. This year we had record amounts of people hear about Jesus in our Easter gatherings at all of our locations. We came together to have an egg hunt and thousands of people came and heard about the Resurrection. Jesus is glorified in unity. Jesus is blessing us in this unification. Maybe you need to ask forgiveness today for being a part of the quarreling in God's family. Maybe you need to ask someone forgiveness for being a part of a church split. I pray for us as a church, regardless of how difficult it is always to be unified in God's Word.

3

WIS-DUMB

Dr. Randy Johnson | Growth Pastor

Do you remember your parents telling you to wait until you are older? What was the topic? ____________________

____

____

In chapter two, Paul continues the discussion of the cross but then addresses issues that are designed for those who are mature (verse 6). How would you identify a mature Christian?

____

____

____

And I, when I came to you, brothers, did not come proclaiming to you the testimony of God with lofty speech or wisdom. 2 For I decided to know nothing among you except Jesus Christ and him crucified. 3 And I was with you in weakness and in fear and much trembling, 4 and my speech and my message were not in plausible words of wisdom, but in demonstration of the Spirit and of power, 5 so that your faith might not rest in the wisdom of men but in the power of God.

Can you summarize Paul's message in five words or less?

____

____

____

Acts 4:13 reads, ***"Now when they saw the boldness of Peter and John, and perceived that they were uneducated, common men, they were astonished. And they recognized that they had been with Jesus."***

Witnessing is just telling your story concerning Jesus. Can you tell your story in 30 seconds (elevator pitch)? ________________

____

____

6 Yet among the mature we do impart wisdom, although it is not a wisdom of this age or of the rulers of this age, who are doomed to pass away. 7 But we impart a secret and hidden wisdom of God, which God decreed before the ages for our glory. 8 None of the rulers of this age understood this, for if they had, they would not have crucified the Lord of glory. 9 But, as it is written, "What no eye has seen, nor ear heard, nor the heart of man imagined, what God has prepared for those who love him"— 10 these things God has revealed to us through the Spirit. For the Spirit searches everything, even the depths of God. 11 For who knows a person's thoughts except the spirit of that person, which is in him? So also no one comprehends the thoughts of God except the Spirit of God. 12 Now we have received not the spirit of the world, but the Spirit who is from God, that we might understand the things freely given us by God. 13 And we impart this in words not taught by human wisdom but

taught by the Spirit, interpreting spiritual truths to those who are spiritual.

What point is Paul making by quoting Isaiah 64:4 (verse 9)?

____

____

____

Jeremiah 29:11 gives another blessing, ***"For I know the plans I have for you, declares the Lord, plans for welfare and not for evil, to give you a future and a hope."***

Write a summary sentence combining verse nine (Isaiah 64:4) and Jeremiah 29:11. _______________________________

____

____

In Colossians 4:14 and Philemon 1:24, Paul includes Demas as part of his entourage greeting other believers. However, 2 Timothy 4:10 starts off, ***"For Demas, in love with this present world, has deserted me and gone to Thessalonica."***

Why do people who seem to have been a follower of Jesus fall away? ____________________________________

____

____

What steps can we take to try and help avoid this?

____

____

____

How does the world define success? ______________________________
____
____

How does God define success? ______________________________
____
____

Realizing Paul's emphasis on unity, Henry Ford's thoughts are interesting, "Coming together is a beginning; keeping together is progress; working together is success."

14 The natural person does not accept the things of the Spirit of God, for they are folly to him, and he is not able to understand them because they are spiritually discerned. 15 The spiritual person judges all things, but is himself to be judged by no one. 16 "For who has understood the mind of the Lord so as to instruct him?" But we have the mind of Christ.

The Holy Spirit

John 14:26 – ***"But the Helper, the Holy Spirit, whom the Father will send in my name, he will teach you all things and bring to your remembrance all that I have said to you."***

John 15:26 – ***"But when the Helper comes, whom I will send to you from the Father, the Spirit of truth, who proceeds from the Father, he will bear witness about me."***

John 16:13-15 – ***"When the Spirit of truth comes, he will guide you into all the truth, for he will not speak on his own authority, but whatever he hears he will speak, and***

he will declare to you the things that are to come. He will glorify me, for he will take what is mine and declare it to you. All that the Father has is mine; therefore I said that he will take what is mine and declare it to you."

1 John 2:27 – ***"But the anointing that you received from him abides in you, and you have no need that anyone should teach you. But as his anointing teaches you about everything, and is true, and is no lie—just as it has taught you, abide in him."***

List some ways the Holy Spirit helps believers.

____

____

____

The mind of Christ

Philippians 2:5 - ***"Have this mind among yourselves, which is yours in Christ Jesus."***

Romans 11:34 - ***"For who has known the mind of the Lord, or who has been his counselor?"***

What does it mean to have the mind of Christ (verse 16)?

____

____

____

How does the work of the Holy Spirit and having the mind of Christ relate back to the previous chapter and the problem with divisions in the church? ______________________

____

THE PRIORITY OF THE GOSPEL

Pastor Scott Johnson | Connections Pastor

1 Corinthians 2:1-2
"And I, when I came to you brothers, did not come proclaiming to you the testimony of God with lofty speech or wisdom. For I decided to know nothing among you except Jesus Christ and him crucified."

I have never been overly involved in politics. However, I do find myself getting caught up in many of the presidential debates. I get intrigued and end up watching for a good amount of time as each candidate banters back and forth about his or her political convictions. As interesting as it may seem, I often find myself asking, "What are they even talking about?" The moderator asks a question, and then after several minutes of responses filled with political jargon, arguments, and attacks, I am even more confused than I was before the debate began. What is the point of all of this?

I think believers in Christ often do a similar thing. We can get caught up in intriguing conversations of Theology, Eschatology, Hermeneutics, Calvinism, Dispensationalism, and many other fancy words. Although there may be a time and place for those conversations, I am just not convinced that it should be the focus, and one step further, it may be distracting some people from what really matters.

As Paul addresses the church in Corinth here in chapter 2, he wanted to let them know what was important. When he first came to them (recorded in Acts 18), he was not concerned with impressing them with his own wisdom. He did not want to confuse them by explaining everything he knew about who God was. It would not have done him any good to debate deep issues of Theology with these people. He was centered on making sure that they understood the Gospel of Jesus Christ. It was his aim to make sure the people understood that they were sinners in need of a Savior and that Savior is Jesus Christ alone.

We as believers have a desire to see lost souls come to know Jesus. When we speak with our neighbors, our friends, and our family members who do not have a relationship with Jesus, we must be careful not to get caught up in lofty words and our own intellect (however limited or extensive that may be). We need to be sure that the saving power of Jesus Christ through His death, burial, and resurrection is what is being heard.

1 CORINTHIANS 2: DEVOTION 2

THE SERIOUSNESS OF THE MISSION

Pastor Scott Johnson | Connections Pastor

---

1 Corinthians 2:3-5
"And I was with you in weakness and in fear and much trembling, and my speech and my message were not plausible words of wisdom, but in demonstration of the Spirit and of power, that your faith might not rest in the wisdom of men but in the power of God."

When I was in college, I was required to take a speech class during my freshman year. The only thing that could have been worse for me at that time was to let a Tarantula crawl on my skin! Yikes! Dropping that class was certainly in the forefront of my mind. However, to eventually graduate, I knew it had to be done. I will never forget the first time I gave a speech in that class. Minutes before it was my turn, my friend looked over at me to see if I was ready. He busted out into laughter as he noticed I had already sweated through a good portion of my shirt under my arms. There was no hiding my fear and trembling!

As much as I hated it at the time, God used that class to help me overcome my fear of public speaking. So now, when I have the opportunity to teach or preach in front of people, can I do it with absolutely no fear, trembling, or anxiety? No. Not even close. However, there is a unique difference between the anxiety I faced in college and the anxiety I have today. I am comfortable speaking in public and being in front of people. It is the weight of the message, the importance of the Scripture, and the seriousness of the mission that makes me tremble. I pray I do not take it too lightly.

Paul had completely surrendered his life to the preaching of the

Gospel. He had planned to give it his all until the day he died. Because of his passion and love for what Jesus had done in his life, he knew the message he preached was incredibly serious. That is why he brought the message, as he says, ***"in weakness and fear and much trembling."*** Paul knew the transforming power that the Gospel of Jesus Christ brings.

It does not matter if you preach the word every day, teach it every week, or simply read and study it on your own. We cannot rely on our own knowledge (lesson 1), and we must understand the weight and the extreme importance of the Scripture.

As believers, we must not rely on the worthless wisdom of man, but rather allow the Spirit to demonstrate God's power. That is our goal!

MAN'S WISDOM V. GOD'S POWER

Pastor Scott Johnson | Connections Pastor

1 Corinthians 2:3-5
"And I was with you in weakness and in fear and much trembling, and my speech and my message were not plausible words of wisdom, but in demonstration of the Spirit and of power, that your faith might not rest in the wisdom of men but in the power of God."

While studying through this chapter in 1 Corinthians, there was a concept that stuck out to me more than the others. That is why I want to revisit the same passage that we looked at in the second devotion. The concept is the wisdom of man and the power of God.

I think we all have had a conversation with the guy who knows all the answers. The guy who must make his flawless opinion known no matter what the subject of the conversation. Be careful not to disagree or correct him because we all know he will not receive it. Ah, yes, the wise guy. Let's be honest, many of us have probably been guilty of being that person at times. So, is it wrong to be filled with knowledge? Is it such a bad thing to share our opinion on a matter? Is it sinful to have intellect and wisdom and want to help teach others what we know? Of course not. However, there is no way we can answer each of those without knowing every detail. However, the intent is worth examining.

This is not the first or the last time the apostle Paul discusses this subject of man's wisdom and knowledge. We can look as closely at the previous chapter as well as the following chapter. 1 Corinthians 1:20b says, ***"Has not God made foolish the wisdom of the world?"*** 1 Corinthians 3:19-20 says, ***"For the wisdom of the world is folly with God. For it is written, 'The***

Lord knows the thoughts of the wise, that they are futile.'"

These are just a few examples in Scripture where God shows the folly of man's idea. The point that Paul wants us to understand is that man cannot get to God on his own. The world is full of ideas, religions, philosophies, strategies, and innovations for man to figure out the meaning of his existence and what matters most. The Bible teaches clearly that man's ways are not God's ways, and that the one and only answer in all of it is Jesus Christ.

In the phrase ***"wisdom of men but in the power of God"*** we see that there are two ideas in complete contrast with each other, and they cannot go together, much like "no one can serve two masters" (Matthew 6). Only one can be the true faith. If your faith rests in the wisdom of man, then that faith is a fraud.

No, it is not necessarily a sin to have knowledge, wisdom, or to want to share your opinion all the time. As a matter of fact, the book of Proverbs often mentions wisdom in a positive way. However, be careful where the emphasis is directed. Ask yourself the question, ***"Am I now seeking the approval of man, or of God? Or am I trying to please man?"*** (Galatians 1:10)

MATURITY

Pastor Scott Johnson | Connections Pastor

---

1 Corinthians 2:6-8
"Yet among the mature we do impart wisdom, although it is not the wisdom of this age or of the rulers of this age, who are doomed to pass away. But we impart a secret and hidden wisdom of God, which God decreed before the ages of our glory. None of the rulers of this age understood it, for if they had, they would not have crucified the Lord of glory."

A typical adult in the United States today probably considers himself or herself to be mature. They get up every morning, eat breakfast, make sure they are dressed properly, get to work on time, and do what they are expected to do at work. Occasionally, they may even go beyond the call of duty and add a little more than the expected. Throughout the month, they pay their bills, maintain their relationships, make sure the family is not neglected and even find time for many different social events and hobbies. With all of this going on, they still are able to make daily decisions, and be a responsible functioning person in society. Some may consider these things to be signs of maturity, and others may disagree completely. That is because we may define the term by our own standards.

So what does it mean to be mature?

Paul shows us in a passage that it is the one who has genuinely believed and trusted in Christ. To show us this, he contrasts with the exact opposite. The rulers were the leaders of the law or those in authority. I would imagine that they would fit the description of someone who is mature. They were responsible for making many decisions on certain issues and were functioning very well in the culture in which they lived. However, they lacked the wisdom to understand that Jesus was the Messiah. They denied Him as the Savior and crucified Him. The gospel is foolishness to them (1 Corinthians 1:21-23).

Are you a believer and a follower in Jesus? If so, we know that we have wisdom through Him. This is not the same thing as the wisdom of man from the previous devotion. There is no reliance on our own power or mind. It is complete maturity to know that we do not have the answers. We can completely rely on Christ for our wisdom.

We can measure a person's true wisdom by whether they recognize Jesus as the Lord of glory.

THE MIND OF CHRIST

Pastor Scott Johnson | Connections Pastor

1 Corinthians 2:16
"For who has understood the mind of the Lord so as to instruct him? But we have the mind of Christ."

When my sons were learning to crawl, the world was full of new things to discover. I would carefully watch them crawl up to the space heater and put their chubby little hand out to touch it, in order to discover the wonders it held. At six months old, they were unaware of the dangers it could hold for them. It was my job to protect them from the danger. I could choose several different ways to protect them. Option number one, I could move them into a different area or move the space heater. Option number two, I could simply tell them "no" firmly. Finally, option number three, I could follow them to the space heater and flick their hand and tell them "DON'T TOUCH! That is hot and will burn you!" Which option is the best for instruction? With option one, they would never know the danger that existed. They would not learn what I know to be true. With option two, it warns them, but without any basis for why they should not perform that behavior. So, they still do not learn what I know to be true. Option three provides a slighter hint of the danger and a clear instruction as to why the space heater was to be left alone, but without experiencing the pain. Thus teaching them what I know to be true.

In this verse, Paul is telling us that God has given us option number three. He quotes Isaiah from the Old Testament. The "mind of the Lord" is referring to an understanding of God's Word, His plan, and His purpose. No one has the ability to know the mind of God except God alone. However, He has given us access through His Word and by the Holy Spirit. Now as believers, we have the "mind" of Christ. This is the consciousness of the scriptures and the ability to perceive and judge. Having the Mind of Christ means we understand God's plan in the world—to bring glory to Himself, restore creation to its original splendor, and provide salvation for sinners. The believer has the ability to understand the Mind of Christ, through the Bible and because we have the Holy Spirit indwelling in us.

Understanding and applying the "Mind of the Lord" is the goal of each believer.

NATURAL V. SPIRITUAL

Pastor Scott Johnson | Connections Pastor

1 Corinthians 2:14-15
"The natural person does not accept the things of the Spirit of God, for they are folly to him, and he is not able to understand them because they are spiritually discerned. The spiritual person judges all things, but is himself to be judged by no one."

As we have been working our way through this chapter, we have been continually looking at the wisdom of God versus the wisdom of man. The next section that Paul discusses is the most practical application for us. He compares the natural man versus the spiritual man.

The natural man is the sinner who has not been saved through grace and has not accepted Jesus as having an active role in his life. He does not lead his life according to the will of God. As I think about this man, I can think of endless examples of where this is evident in our world. The natural man seeks as much personal gain as he can. He says live the lifestyle that makes you happy. He says your body is your own, and you can choose what you do with it. These are just a few things that are in direct opposition of what the spiritual man knows as truth. These are the lies that Satan has told the natural man. Paul describes these 'wisdoms' as folly.

The spiritual man lives in direct opposition to the natural man. He is the man that seeks to follow after God's heart because he has been saved from his justly deserved death from sin. He is the man that seeks to be obedient to what God asks of us in His Word. Where the natural man says to build up personal gain, the spiritual man says that God declares what good is it to gain the whole world yet lose his soul. The natural man says I can live the lifestyle that feels right to me, but the spiritual man says God has shown me the standard that is most profitable to live by. The natural man says his body is his own, but the spiritual man says his body is the temple of God and he must treat it accordingly. The priorities of the spiritual man are set upon the glory of God, and the natural man's are set upon the glory of himself.

Paul states here that the spiritual man is to judge all things. As believers in Christ, we are to hold all things up to the light of the scripture to see whether they are profitable or not. When we use that as our guide, we do not need to worry about the judgment of man. We will be pleasing the ultimate Judge that we will one day answer to about the wisdom we followed while here on earth. Satan is continually trying to get us to follow the folly of man's wisdom, but if we want to live worthy of our gift of salvation we have been freely given, then we must use the wisdom of God as the standard by which we live.

4

PARISH OR PERISH?

Dr. Randy Johnson | Growth Pastor

This chapter is similar to Hebrews 5:11-14, ***"About this we have much to say, and it is hard to explain, since you have become dull of hearing. For though by this time you ought to be teachers, you need someone to teach you again the basic principles of the oracles of God. You need milk, not solid food, for everyone who lives on milk is unskilled in the word of righteousness, since he is a child. But solid food is for the mature, for those who have their powers of discernment trained by constant practice to distinguish good from evil."***

There are two kinds of people – Christians and unsaved. There are two kinds of Christians – mature and immature (carnal). From Hebrews 5, what is the mark of a mature believer?

____

____

____

"What makes Superman a hero is not that he has power, but that he has the wisdom and the maturity to use the power wisely." Christopher Reeve

But I, brothers, could not address you as spiritual people, but as people of the flesh, as infants in Christ. 2 I fed you with milk, not solid food, for you were not ready for it. And even now you are not yet ready, 3 for you are still of the flesh. For while there is jealousy and strife among you, are you not of the flesh and behaving only in a human way? 4 For when one says, "I follow Paul," and another, "I follow Apollos," are you not being merely human?

If freedom from jealousy and quarreling (verse 3) is a mark of Christian maturity, how would you evaluate your own maturity in Christ? ____

____

____

Preachers have different styles. What distinction should be made between preference and conviction? ______________________

____

____

5 What then is Apollos? What is Paul? Servants through whom you believed, as the Lord assigned to each. 6 I planted, Apollos watered, but God gave the growth. 7 So neither he who plants nor he who waters is anything, but only God who gives the growth. 8 He who plants and he who waters are one, and each will receive his wages according to his labor. 9 For we are God's fellow workers. You are God's field, God's building.

Did Paul, Apollos, and Cephas have problems with each other?

____

____

____

How have you seen people try to create division among leaders (ie. Children with parents)? ______________________________

____

____

How does Paul use a farming metaphor to convey his point?

____

____

____

10 According to the grace of God given to me, like a skilled master builder I laid a foundation, and someone else is building upon it. Let each one take care how he builds upon it. 11 For no one can lay a foundation other than that which is laid, which is Jesus Christ. 12 Now if anyone builds on the foundation with gold, silver, precious stones, wood, hay, straw— 13 each one's work will become manifest, for the Day will disclose it, because it will be revealed by fire, and the fire will test what sort of work each one has done. 14 If the work that anyone has built on the foundation survives, he will receive a reward. 15 If anyone's work is burned up, he will suffer loss, though he himself will be saved, but only as through fire.

How does Paul use a building metaphor to convey his point?

____

____

____

Matthew 7:24-27 says, ***"Everyone then who hears these words of mine and does them will be like a wise man who built his house on the rock. And the rain fell, and the floods came, and the winds blew and beat on that house, but it did not***

fall, because it had been founded on the rock. And everyone who hears these words of mine and does not do them will be like a foolish man who built his house on the sand. And the rain fell, and the floods came, and the winds blew and beat against that house, and it fell, and great was the fall of it."

What foundation is used by different people for his or her life? What should be our foundation? ______________________________

____

____

Even the fairy tale, The Three Little Pigs, displays the value of building materials.

16 Do you not know that you are God's temple and that God's Spirit dwells in you? 17 If anyone destroys God's temple, God will destroy him. For God's temple is holy, and you are that temple.

As you think about your own Christian community, what does it mean that you are God's temple (verse 16)? ____________________

____

____

Is God's temple and its outworking the responsibility of ministers or all believers? ____

____

____

18 Let no one deceive himself. If anyone among you thinks that he is wise in this age, let him become a fool that he may become wise. 19 For the wisdom of this world is folly with God. For it is written, "He catches the wise in their

craftiness," 20 and again, "The Lord knows the thoughts of the wise, that they are futile." 21 So let no one boast in men. For all things are yours, 22 whether Paul or Apollos or Cephas or the world or life or death or the present or the future—all are yours, 23 and you are Christ's, and Christ is God's.

When have you had to discard the wisdom of the world in order to be open to receive God's wisdom (verse 18)? ________________

____

____

Consider the vast areas which Paul names in verse 22 – the world, life, death, the present, the future. What does it mean that they all are yours because you belong to Christ? ________________

____

____

WISE UP!

Pastor Ty Woznek | Pastor's Academy Lead Instructor

Choose to pursue Jesus.

There was an elderly professor who was profoundly boring. His reputation preceded him, and my heart sank when he taught church history. Plain spoken, no flash. Dull. I was wrong. What he taught me was humility, love, and a heartbeat for the church. The term 'unification' that is used at The River started with that man. What changed was the second day of class. That evening he walked along Schroon Lake holding his wife's hand, sat on a bench, and the two kissed. There was something more to that man.

Today's devotional may sting a little. Christians often fear theology. They believe the practical or immediate outweighs thoughtfulness. It creates a climate where personalities or preferences matter more than pursuing Jesus.

Paul says, ***"But I, brothers, could not address you as spiritual people, but as people of the flesh, as infants in Christ. I fed you with milk, not solid food, for you were not ready for it. And even now you are not yet ready, for you are still of the flesh. For while there is jealousy and strife among you, are you not of the flesh and behaving only in a human way? For when one says, 'I follow Paul,' and another, 'I follow Apollos,' are you not being merely human?"***

That is labeling!

In my first year of pastoral ministry, my teenagers were mad about labeling. I set up a potluck soup lunch for the next week. Each person brought a can of soup to my office. We would each grab a can, and that would be our lunch. Here is the problem: I removed all labels, and I added four cans of dog food. I mentioned that fact when they were about to grab a can to eat. Suddenly labels had value. We have a label. (My wife had pizza on hand. Jesus has forgiveness and grace.)

Time to rebrand

Paul grills the believers at Corinth to rebrand themselves. They needed to grow up spiritually. Paul gives us three labels:

Natural: a person who did ask Jesus to save them by believing that Jesus died and rose again for their sin.

Fleshly: An immature Christian, who is not rooted in the things of God, results in a self-focus.

Spiritual: A person, who through practice is mindful of the Bible and how he interacts with others, resulting in humility.

What label are you?

Your label shows

How you get along with others reveals your label. One who digs into the Bible to learn what it says will act remarkably different from one who does not. If you are abrasive, jealous, create conflict, claim favorites, write off other people, or lack gratitude, then you are an immature Christian. This does not mean God is finished with you; it means you need to change and wise up. Yes, this stings, but it does not have to be the end of your story! The person you undervalue the most may have the most to offer you!

THINK TEAM

Pastor Ty Woznek | Pastor's Academy Lead Instructor

We have tunnel vision.

While trying an experiment with children, teenagers, and adults, they all failed because of tunnel vision. The task was fairly simple. I wanted them to build a single tower as high as they could using their Legos. Immediately, each person built a tower as high as he or she could. I told them they failed, repeated my instructions, and the towers changed. After about the third or fourth time, they realized they could work together. (Kids often got this before the adults did.)

Paul says, ***"What then is Apollos? What is Paul? Servants through whom you believed, as the Lord assigned to each. I planted, Apollos watered, but God gave the growth. So neither he who plants nor he who waters is anything, but only God who gives the growth. He who plants and he who waters are one, and each will receive his wages according to his labor. For we are God's fellow workers. You are God's field, God's building."***

Church is a team sport

Paul describes the church (that is you and me who are in Christ), as a farm and as a building. The concept is a work in progress. Too often, we get tunnel vision and think church is individual and not team, not family. The word church comes from a Greek word that means "a group of people gathered together for a purpose." Our gathering together is to grow in the Word so we can reach people with the Gospel. When you see the word "church" think "Gospel Team." (Oh, I read the end of the Bible, and we win!)

Get to work

We like to be like our favorites and fear being ourselves. God designed and placed us for a reason. I struggle with not being an evangelist. I would love to be one if I could choose any gift in the Bible. Why? I want people to get to know Jesus. However, God did not make me an evangelist; he made me a teacher. I found that when I did what God designed me to do, people were reached with the Gospel, just not by me. What changed my heart was seeing that it is a team. The team won a person. Find your role and do it with all your might!

God can, God does

Ultimately, God is the one who causes growth. God is the one saves. God is the one who puts our team together. God doing the work does not mean we sit on the sidelines and watch. It means we put our hand up and say "put me in the game!" My first pastor put it this way: "We can do nothing and expect God to work, or we can do our best and expect God to work just the same." Appreciate what others do, but get in the game. We need you.

IF YOU BUILD IT...

Pastor Ty Woznek | Pastor's Academy Lead Instructor

You better be careful.

Careful is not always a matter of fear, but it is always a matter of focus. Anniversary dates are important to my wife, so I am careful to plan for them. We are careful with what is important to us. Importance drives focus.

Paul says, ***"According to the grace of God given to me, like a skilled master builder I laid a foundation, and someone else is building upon it. Let each one take care how he builds upon it. For no one can lay a foundation other than that which is laid, which is Jesus Christ."***

Get building!

It is not a matter of if you are a builder. It is a matter of how good of a builder you are. You and I are theologians. You and I are missionaries. It is a matter of how good we know God's Word or how intentional we are to reach people for Jesus. Paul is asking us how intentional, how careful, are we in building Christ's church?

Foundation is set

We lay a foundation once. Our foundation is Jesus. Other passages call Him the cornerstone by which the whole building is measured and aligned. Jesus is an unshakable, unwavering platform to build, and you and I get to build on that foundation! Paul, again, is reminding us it is all about Jesus.

Others' sacrifice

You are a part of the Body of Christ. You are reading a copy of God's Word in your language. You are reading out of a booklet (or online). All that was done based on the work of another. The work we did was based on the work of others. The work they did is based on the work of another. Some of these others died so you and I could read and know God's Word. Others gave sacrificially.

What are you building?
Get in the game. Build. Build well. Others in the future need you to do your part. You ARE a builder of Christ's church. Be a good one.

GO FOR GOLD!

Pastor Ty Woznek | Pastor's Academy Lead Instructor

I got in trouble...

Apparently shooting a projectile across the science lab is a punishable offense. (We missed our target by two centimeters!) Given the choice of suspension via the principal or joining the Science Olympiad team, I chose the extra work (and my dad not knowing why). The teacher saw the potential to beat a rival school. We were smart enough to get in trouble, so she put us to more "constructive accomplishments. After all, physics is fun." It was sweeter to be the first in my school to win a key event. Life lesson: Winning is not always winning.

Paul says, ***"Now if anyone builds on the foundation with gold, silver, precious stones, wood, hay, straw-- each one's work will become manifest, for the Day will disclose it, because it will be revealed by fire, and the fire will test what sort of work each one has done. If the work that anyone has built on the foundation survives, he will receive a reward. If anyone's work is burned up, he will suffer loss, though he himself will be saved, but only as through fire."***

Quality of our ministry

Jesus will judge us on the quality of our ministry, not on our sin. He paid for our sins on the cross. As we said earlier, you ARE a builder of Christ's church. The matter is how good of a builder are you. Here the issue is not good versus evil, but of better versus best. We must evaluate ourselves and be the best God designed us to be. We must not be slothful in building the church, but highly engaged.

Once saved, always saved

Once you are in Christ, you are going to heaven. However, that does not mean you will be rewarded. When I graduated high school, some were thrilled that they JUST passed with a 64.5 %. Others were thrilled at honors they received for their high GPA. The testing will purify our work. Work to excel, not merely pass into heaven.

No sidelines

There are no sidelines to the church. So, if you are not actively, intentionally engaged in building Christ's church, why? Either in your growth community or with a trusted mentor ask about getting in the game. Not just because we need you, but also so you can go for the gold!

WARNING

Pastor Ty Woznek | Pastor's Academy Lead Instructor

Paul says, ***"Do you not know that you are God's temple and that God's Spirit dwells in you? If anyone destroys God's temple, God will destroy him. For God's temple is holy, and you are that temple."***

You are moving either forward or backward. There is no maintaining. You are either building Christ's church, or you are hurting it. There is no such thing as a "pew warmer" (a person who just attends). This may seem harsh or even sound legalistic, but the Bible is clear about our involvement in building the church. The church is people, not the physical location we meet.

No demolitionists

Paul grilled the Corinthians for their immaturity because it was hurting the church. Jesus died and gave Himself up for the church. Grace and mercy were not cheap; it cost God His best: Jesus. When we do not get along well with other Christians, or when we do not bother to help build up other Christians, we are hurting the church. Period.

Not building, try this

- Find someone who loves Jesus, and ask him or her to help you do the same!
- Get into a Growth Community with other believers you can learn from.
- If you have offended another Christian, go to that person and make it right.
- Make gatherings about others and not about you. If everyone goes to church focused on meeting everyone's needs, everyone's needs get met.

- Right now, call, email, text a pastor or ministry leader, and ask how you can help.
- Get on your knees and pray for others, for your church, for people who do not know Jesus, and be specific.
- Purpose in your heart that building the church is a vital part of your life.

Ok, ok, ok, I'm doing these things
For those who are spiritual and this week has not been your struggle, seek those out who do struggle. The purpose of those who are spiritual is to nurture and guide those who are not. Building Christ's church is not reach, gather, grow, and arrived. It is back to reach, back to gather, back to grow, reach more, gather more, grow more, etc. When you and I see Jesus face to face, then our work is done.

1 CORINTHIANS 3: DEVOTION 6

DEFINE YOUR ROCK

Pastor Ty Woznek | Pastor's Academy Lead Instructor

JUMP!

NO! Let's be honest, the water was way over my head, and my family was filled with practical jokesters. The St. Lawrence Seaway was a river. Rivers have currents. I'm a skinny kid that could get blown away by 3 MPH winds. Clearly, my aunt was not my rock, even if she did have a really big lifejacket on. Yeah, I was that wimpy kid.

Paul says, ***"Let no one deceive himself. If anyone among you thinks that he is wise in this age, let him become a fool that he may become wise. For the wisdom of this world is folly with God. For it is written, 'He catches the wise in their craftiness,' and again, 'The Lord knows the thoughts of the wise, that they are futile.' So let no one boast in men. For all things are yours, whether Paul or Apollos or Cephas or the world or life or death or the present or the future--all are yours, and you are Christ's, and Christ is God's."***

We want idols; we want kings

Want to make your pastors happy? Pursue Jesus as your rock. Like Israel, we want a king over us. We just call them pastors in the church, or Smile FM, or our favorite speaker, or our methodology (yes, pastors struggle too). An idol is something that replaces God. We do that all the time. The Corinthians relied on their leaders more than they relied on Jesus. They idolized them. We do the same.

Your pastor is not that great

Your pastor is not everywhere. Your pastor does not know everything. Your pastor is not perfect, quite the opposite. Now, why would the Bible talk about listening to and honoring pastors if you pastor is not that great? This is because Jesus is great, and Jesus is our Head Pastor. Pastors are to feed us the Word of God and lead us to reach people, but pastors cannot sustain us. Only Jesus can. Pastors cannot save us. Only Jesus can. Pastors are not God, only God is. Jesus has to be our rock, our focus.

A great pastor is humble

What made Paul, Apollos, or Cephas great was their pursuit of Jesus. They fulfilled the ministry that God called them to. They were a team. I have had the privilege to work with great pastors. The key ingredient to a great pastor is humility. We need to understand that as we work as hard as we can, Jesus is the one who causes growth. The win for great pastors is people seeing and pursuing Jesus. As Paul says, we are here to serve you and build you, the church, up in Christ. However, we are not your rock, Jesus is!

Define your rock

What is your foundation? Are you building on that foundation? Those are the questions 1 Corinthians 3 is asking us. It has to be about Jesus. If it is about Jesus, then we have to be humble like Jesus was humble. We appreciate the work of others, but we also roll up our sleeves and work as well.

5

PUFFED OR POWERFUL?

Dr. Randy Johnson | Growth Pastor

Paul strives to minister before an audience of One – God! He tries to avoid letting negative tones and complimentary notes affect his known purpose, calling, and ministry.

Which better describes your view of ministry:

Pastor – actor, God – prompter, congregation – critics?

Pastor – prompter, God – critic, congregation – actors?

This is how one should regard us, as servants of Christ and stewards of the mysteries of God. 2 Moreover, it is required of stewards that they be found faithful. 3 But with me it is a very small thing that I should be judged by you or by any human court. In fact, I do not even judge myself. 4 For I am not aware of anything against myself, but I am not thereby acquitted. It is the Lord who judges me. 5 Therefore do not pronounce judgment before the time, before the Lord comes, who will bring to light the things now hidden in darkness and will disclose the purposes of the heart. Then each one will receive his commendation from God.

Instead of boasting about some leaders and criticizing others, how should Christians view their leaders (verse 1)?

___

___

___

What does it mean to be stewards of the mysteries of God?

___

___

___

How do these verse relate to Galatians 1:10, ***"For am I now seeking the approval of man, or of God? Or am I trying to please man? If I were still trying to please man, I would not be a servant of Christ"***? ___

___

___

What is the difference between having a "clear conscience" and being "innocent"? ___

___

___

What word did you expect in verse 5 commendation or condemnation? ___

___

___

6 I have applied all these things to myself and Apollos for your benefit, brothers, that you may learn by us not to go beyond what is written, that none of you may be puffed up in favor of one against another. 7 For who sees anything different in you? What do you have that you did not receive?

If then you received it, why do you boast as if you did not receive it?

Fantasy sports' site FanDuel is now worth over $1 billion. It can be a consuming hobby for many, but we need to make sure we don't create "Fantasy church" picking certain pastors instead of being the church.

Was their pride based in their leaders or in themselves? Explain.

___

___

___

The verb be puffed up (literally, "be inflated") is used 6 times in 1 Corinthians (4:6, 18-19; 5:2; 8:1; 13:4), but only once in his other writings. Boast also occurs frequently (1:29, 31; 3:21; 4:7). How can one strive to overcome an unhealthy pride?

___

___

___

How would you answer the question in verse seven, For who sees anything different in you? Or what do people see different in you?

___

___

___

8 Already you have all you want! Already you have become rich! Without us you have become kings! And would that you did reign, so that we might share the rule with you! 9 For I think that God has exhibited us apostles as last of all, like men sentenced to death, because we have become a spectacle to the world, to angels, and to men. 10 We are

fools for Christ's sake, but you are wise in Christ. We are weak, but you are strong. You are held in honor, but we in disrepute. 11 To the present hour we hunger and thirst, we are poorly dressed and buffeted and homeless, 12 and we labor, working with our own hands. When reviled, we bless; when persecuted, we endure; 13 when slandered, we entreat. We have become, and are still, like the scum of the world, the refuse of all things.

The word spectacle (verse 9) is the idea of being on display. Look forward to verse 20 and compare the concepts.

____

____

____

How in verses 10-13 do you see the crucified Messiah as Paul's model for ministry? ______________________________

____

____

How would Paul respond to the idea popular today, "God wants you to be happy, rich, and successful"? __________________

____

____

Rick Warren has said, "I don't think it is a sin to be rich. I think it is a sin to die rich." What do you think? ________________

____

____

14 I do not write these things to make you ashamed, but to admonish you as my beloved children. 15 For though you have countless guides in Christ, you do not have many

fathers. For I became your father in Christ Jesus through the gospel. 16 I urge you, then, be imitators of me. 17 That is why I sent you Timothy, my beloved and faithful child in the Lord, to remind you of my ways in Christ, as I teach them everywhere in every church. 18 Some are arrogant, as though I were not coming to you. 19 But I will come to you soon, if the Lord wills, and I will find out not the talk of these arrogant people but their power. 20 For the kingdom of God does not consist in talk but in power. 21 What do you wish? Shall I come to you with a rod, or with love in a spirit of gentleness?

Paul, who founded the Corinthian family (verses 14-15), was an example for his spiritual children (verses 16-17) and was willing to discipline his spiritual children (verses 18-21).

What do you think of this phrase: There are no grandchildren in Heaven, only children? ________________________________

____

____

Do you have someone you would refer to as a spiritual father or mother? ____

____

____

What does it take to be a spiritual father or mother?

____

____

____

Does verse 21 give only an either or scenario, or can there be a time to use both approaches together? ____________________

Remember: The only thing you can take to Heaven is a friend.

SELECTED SHEPHERDS

Philip Piasecki | Worship Leader

Allow me to set the stage. You show up to a weekend gathering, and the Pastor gets up on stage and delivers his message. During the middle of it, you start feeling like he is speaking directly to you. By the end of the sermon, you are completely convicted about a sin in your life. On the drive home, your mind starts to race with thoughts, "Well the Pastor isn't perfect either", "What right does he have to tell me that I am in the wrong?", "I can't believe how he completely lost his train of thought during his second point", and so on and so forth. We have all had this experience in our lives. God uses the Pastor in our life and instead of examining ourselves; we deflect that feeling of conviction.

The believers in Corinth were dealing with some maturity issues and falling into the trap of exalting certain leaders in the church over other ones. Paul addresses this issue in chapter 3 and then continues to look at it deeper in chapter 4. In verses 1-5, Paul takes the opportunity to speak on how He operates as a Pastor and how believers are supposed to regard the Pastors in their lives. Pastors have been entrusted with the great responsibility of sharing the mysteries of God (verse 1) with people. Paul explains that it is his responsibility to make sure he is found trustworthy and that he understands God will judge him one day to make sure he was a good steward of what God had given him.

As believers, we need to understand this passage in a way that affects how we behave. Let's look back at the story from the beginning of this devotional. Many of us have had a very similar experience to that story. When that happened, did we respond in a Godly manner? We need to understand that God has placed the Pastors in our lives in authority over us. They are servants of Christ, who will one day answer to God for how they led their sheep. So, when they speak truth into our lives, we need to allow the Holy Spirit to use their words to convict us. When we feel the convicting of the Holy Spirit through the Pastor's words, we need to respond accordingly. The responsibilities of Pastors are great, as is our biblical responsibility towards those Pastors God has placed in our lives. Let's not lose focus of the fact that God has placed specific pastoral leadership in our lives for a reason. Instead, let's allow the Holy Spirit to use that leadership to further sanctify us in our walks with Christ

TEAM WORKS

Philip Piasecki | Worship Leader

For the last two years, I have coached 7th grade basketball at Brandon Middle School. As I am sure many of you know, middle school boys are some of the strangest people on the planet. Figuring out how to interact with them, let alone teach them basketball, can be an impossible task. One of my main goals for the season was to help these kids understand that everyone has an important role on the team. From our star player to the last kid off the bench, they all had an important role. This concept is a tough one to grasp; they all want to be the kid scoring all the points. The kids scoring all the points thought they were more important than the other kids on the team were. It was a battle every day to stress that each player's role is vital to the success of the team.

Paul finds himself in a similar situation while addressing the Christians in Corinth. The church was seriously struggling with an issue of pride. God blessed the believers there with many different gifts, and instead of being humble and thankful for those gifts, they were boasting about them. Not only were they prideful, but also they were considering themselves or others with certain gifts as better than other believers in the church. They started to view their gifts and abilities as more important than the ones other believers possessed. Paul rebukes these believers and reminds them that God is the one who has given them what they have! They should not be prideful about gifts that they are not responsible for acquiring.

1 Peter 4:10 says, ***"As each has received a gift, use it to serve one another, as good stewards of God's varied grace:"*** As believers we need to understand that God has given us spiritual

gifts to serve each other, not so we can boast. Just like my basketball team, we need to understand that no Christian is "better" than any other one because of the abilities he or she has. God has specifically equipped each believer for the furtherance of His kingdom. The Body of Christ is a team, and each member plays a vital role. We cannot let pride fill our hearts and minds. If we ever feel that we are struggling with pride, we need to remember 1 Corinthians 4:7. We have nothing that God has not given to us. Whatever spiritual gift or skill you possess was given to you through Christ and the Holy Spirit; use it to serve one another.

LAVISH LIVING

Philip Piasecki | Worship Leader

In 1 Corinthians 4:8 Paul brings a very interesting and touchy subject about the Christians in Corinth to light. He sees that the Christians in Corinth were living very lavish lives here on earth. He explains to them that they are already living like kings here on earth. Paul was upset with them because they seemed to have lost their heavenly perspective. Instead of living their lives with eternity in mind, they were more concerned with living like kings now. Paul knows that one day all believers are going to reign with Christ in eternity, 2 Timothy 2:11-12 says, ***"The saying is trustworthy, for: If we have died with him, we will also live with him; if we endure, we will also reign with him; if we deny him, he also will deny us."*** One day we will reign alongside Christ, but Paul knew he needed to correct how the Corinthian church was living on earth. The Corinthian church was essentially using God as a "get out of jail free card," accepting Him for His salvation, but not wanting to live sacrificially for Him here on earth.

This verse is packed with application to our lives as modern day believers. Luke 12:34 says, ***"For where your treasure is, there will your heart be also."*** We have to understand that being rich is not a sin. There are countless people in the Bible who were very wealthy, and God uses them in mighty ways. Abraham, Solomon, and David are a few examples of very wealthy men who were used in incredible ways by God. However, it becomes sin when wealthy is more important in our heart than Christ is. We will know it is more important to us based on how we are living our lives. If the majority of our time is spent trying to get rich, instead of blessing others with what God has given us, the condition of our heart becomes very clear. That was the issue with the church in

Corinth; they wanted to live like kings here on earth, instead of being selfless, as Christ has called them to be. While on earth, it is important to believers to have an eternal perspective. This place is not our permanent home. If we are lucky we will live on this earth for around eighty years, then we will spend eternity in heaven! I love the illustration where you draw a dot on a piece of paper, and then draw a line from that dot as long as you can. The dot is our life here on earth, and the rest of that line is our eternity in heaven! When we put it into perspective, we can understand why it is so important to live our lives now with eternity in mind. Let us use our time, talent, and money here on earth to impact people for the Gospel. If God chooses to bless us with earthly things, let's use those to bless others. We need to be less concerned about living like kings on earth, and more concerned about heavenly things. With the salvation of our friends and family hanging in the balance, let us make eternity our focus every day.

ROLE MODELS

Philip Piasecki | Worship Leader

In preparation for my wife and I to have our first child, I started thinking a lot about what being a father was all about. I kept coming back to this idea of being an example to my daughter. I know in a couple of years that she is going to be old enough to start imitating me. Eventually, she will be able to repeat words she hears me saying or imitate the actions she sees me performing every day. It really makes you stop and think about what you are doing when you know there are those little pair of eyes following you around watching your every move! My hope is that I can always be a good example to her and that she can learn many positive things just from watching how I behave.

This idea of being an example is something that Paul references here in 1 Corinthians 4:9-13. The whole chapter he talks about what the apostles' ministry looks like and in verses nine he explains that God has "exhibited" the apostles and that they have become a "spectacle to the world." What Paul is saying is that the world looks to the apostles as examples; he understands that their every action is under close watch by people in the church, and those who do not believe in Christ. He continues in verses 10-13 to show some of the ways that they have had to be examples. When we read these verses, it certainly does not sound like a walk in the park! Paul describes them being poorly dressed, homeless, being reviled, being persecuted, and being considered the scum of the world. However, in the midst of that Paul explains that the apostles were able to bless others and endure those situations. The testimony of the apostles is so powerful, and as believers, it is something that we need to take notice of.

Paul understood that they needed to be an example to the church and non-believers. Their every action was under the microscope because of who they were, and not much has changed for us today. We need to understand that every day there are people who see our actions and are influenced by them. Within the body of Christ, other believers will observe how we behave and model themselves after it. So many young believers in the church need someone to show him or her a good example of what a follower of Christ looks like. Outside of the church, we all know people who are watching our actions because they know that we are Christians. So many people are waiting for an opportunity to say, "I can't believe they did that, they told me they were a Christian!" We need our behavior to further support our claims of believing in Jesus Christ. Just as Paul and the apostles were a "spectacle to the world," those around us also are watching us. We need to strive every day to make sure our actions are Godly example to those people who see us every day.

SURROUND YOURSELF

Philip Piasecki | Worship Leader

I have been very blessed to be a Christian since a young age, and to grow up in the church all my life. When I look back over the years of my walk with Christ, I am blown away by the people God has placed in my life to help me grow and mature as a believer. My parents made a decision to invest in me spiritually any chance they got, always doing their best to point me towards Christ. I had youth pastors who valued me enough to disciple me to help me grow in my faith. Still to this day, I have people in my life who are invested in seeing me grow spiritually. These different people have never shied away from admonishing me when they noticed that my actions were contrary to Scripture. They have never done it to embarrass me or to make me feel bad about myself; they did it because they care about my walk with Christ and want to see it continue to grow as a believer.

In 1 Corinthians 4:14-17 Paul deals with this truth with the church in Corinth. He has just finished making them aware of the sinful ways that they are living their lives. He tells them in verse 14 that he is not telling them these things to make them feel ashamed, but to admonish them as his own children. He continues to explain that he has taken the role of being their earthly spiritual father through the Gospel. Anybody who has kids knows that you reprimand your children because you love them, and you want to see them change their ways. This is why Paul uses the analogy of a father and children. He loves the people of the church in Corinth so much that he is willing to be stern with them and speak harshly to them when needed. He knows that they need someone who is willing to speak truth and love into their lives and someone that they can model their Christianity after. Even though Paul was not able to go back and visit the

Corinthian church, he sends Timothy so that he can continue to teach them in the ways of the Scripture. Paul's ultimate desire was that the church in Corinth would continue to mature in their faith every day.

This is such an important truth for us to learn. Many of the Christians in Corinth were a mess, but they allowed Paul to speak truth into their lives when he needed to. We all need to be humble enough to surround ourselves with people who can admonish us when we need it. The body of Christ is a family; we need to find those people who are willing to love and admonish us like their spiritual children. There is always someone who is more mature in his or her faith than you or I. We need to diligently seek those people out and ask them to help us grow into more mature believers. When our spiritual mothers and fathers do reprimand us for our behaviors, we need to be humble enough to accept that reproof. None of us have our walk with Christ 100% figured out, let's be willing to let other mature believers help us figure it out.

WORDS AND ACTIONS

Philip Piasecki | Worship Leader

I have been married now for almost three years. I have learned many lessons over those three years, some the easy way and some the hard way! I have learned the importance of both words and actions. It is so important that I tell my wife every day that I love her. I make sure to tell her that she looks beautiful and that she is important to me. As important as those words are, my actions towards her are even more crucial. If I tell her I love her, but I am mean to her all the time, those words lose their meaning very quickly. If I tell her she is important to me, but I never set time aside to spend with her, those words feel empty. I can be arrogant and say that I am the best husband in the known world, but if my actions do not reflect that, then my words are empty.

Paul deals with this issue with the church in Corinth in 1 Corinthians 4:18-21. The Christians there were being arrogant thinking that Paul was never going to visit the church to address the issues that they were having. Paul says he will come soon and ***"find out not the talk of these arrogant people but their power."*** Essentially, what he was saying is he is going to come to see if their actions back up their words. Paul explains that the kingdom of God does not consist of talk but in power. The Corinthian church was very proud proclaiming what God was doing in the church. Paul explains that he will come soon to find out if they are just proud, or if the power of God is actually working in their lives.

As believers, we need to be very careful that we have substance in our walk with Christ, not just words. If our relationship with Christ is only based on what we say, and not our actions, then we have completely missed it. If you say you love Jesus and then live contrary to that every single day, you may not actually know Christ at all. Our actions cannot save us; we cannot earn salvation through works. However, if we really are Christians, then our actions will reflect that belief! I always think of the Pharisees who knew all the right words to say, but Jesus knew their real spiritual condition. Jesus says in Matthew 24:27, ***"Woe to you, scribes and Pharisees, hypocrites! For you are like whitewashed tombs, which outwardly appear beautiful, but within are full of dead people's bones and all uncleanness."*** The Pharisees knew how to look and sound the part, but inside they were as dead men! Every day we need to honor and glorify Christ with our actions as well as our words. Let us never allow ourselves to be arrogant as the Corinthians were, but humble ourselves and devote our actions to Christ each and every day.

6

SATAN'S SERVANT

Dr. Randy Johnson | Growth Pastor

Paul now speaks on two relevant, but often avoided, topics: sex boundaries and church discipline. It can be good to remember that someone is applauding our thoughts, words, and actions. It is either God or Satan. Paul makes it clear that God is displeased with this inappropriate sexual relationship, but also with how it is not confronted by other believers.

Should these topics be discussed more, less, or just as they are in church and growth communities? ____________________________

____

____

It is actually reported that there is sexual immorality among you, and of a kind that is not tolerated even among pagans, for a man has his father's wife. 2 And you are arrogant! Ought you not rather to mourn? Let him who has done this be removed from among you.

What was the sex scandal (verse 1)? ____________________________

____

____

Was this type of sexual union accepted in the community (verse 1)? ____

____

____

How did the church respond to such behavior (verse 2)?

____

____

____

Based on Matthew 18:15-17 ***("If your brother sins against you, go and tell him his fault, between you and him alone. If he listens to you, you have gained your brother. But if he does not listen, take one or two others along with you, that every charge may be established by the evidence of two or three witnesses. If he refuses to listen to them, tell it to the church. And if he refuses to listen even to the church, let him be to you as a Gentile and a tax collector."), how should the believers have responded to this man?***

"God created us in his image, male and female, with personhood and sexual passions, so that when he comes to us in this world there would be these powerful words and images to describe the promises and the pleasures of our covenant relationship with him through Christ." John Piper

3 For though absent in body, I am present in spirit; and as if present, I have already pronounced judgment on the one who did such a thing. 4 When you are assembled in the name of the Lord Jesus and my spirit is present, with the power of our Lord Jesus, 5 you are to deliver this man to Satan for the destruction of the flesh, so that his spirit may be saved in the day of the Lord.

How would you paraphrase what Paul tells them to do?

How would you describe what had happened to a neighbor who is not a believer?

What is the ultimate goal of this discipline?

What is the concern of not addressing open sin among believers?

6 Your boasting is not good. Do you not know that a little leaven leavens the whole lump? 7 Cleanse out the old leaven that you may be a new lump, as you really are unleavened. For Christ, our Passover lamb, has been sacrificed. 8 Let us therefore celebrate the festival, not with the old leaven, the leaven of malice and evil, but with the unleavened bread of sincerity and truth.

Later in this epistle (15:33), Paul says, ***"Do not be deceived: 'Bad company ruins good morals.'"*** Do you agree that negative influences tend to outweigh positive?

Psalm 1:1 shows a descending process, ***"Blessed is the man who walks not in the counsel of the wicked, nor stands in the way of sinners, nor sits in the seat of scoffers."*** List an example of how this happens in our lives today.

Sincerity and truth (verse 8) implies purity of motive and purity of action. How do these traits relate to our daily life?

---

9 I wrote to you in my letter not to associate with sexually immoral people—10 not at all meaning the sexually immoral of this world, or the greedy and swindlers, or idolaters, since then you would need to go out of the world. 11 But now I am writing to you not to associate with anyone who bears the name of brother if he is guilty of sexual immorality or greed, or is an idolater, reviler, drunkard, or swindler—not even to eat with such a one. 12 For what have I to do with judging outsiders? Is it not those inside the church whom you are to judge? 13 God judges those outside. "Purge the evil person from among you."

The church cannot ignore sin. Paul uses strong words in giving his instructions: be removed (verse 2), deliver this man to Satan (verse 5), cleanse out (verse 7) and purge the evil person (verse 13). Why is he so strong in his comments?

Do Paul's instructions on discipline apply for both believers and unbelievers? Why or why not? ______________________________

____

____

Does this passage disagree with the statement, ***"Be in the world, but not of the world"***? ____________________________________

____

____

"Discipline is something we despise for the moment.... We all look for a place to run, an excuse with which to stall. No one enjoys it. Yet those of us who have endured it know that the fruit it produces and the pain from which it ultimately spares us makes it worth the agony." Charles Stanley

A BLIND EYE

Josue Rodriguez | Pastor's Academy

"It is actually reported that there is sexual immorality among you, and a kind that is not even tolerated among pagans, for a man has his father's wife. And you are arrogant! Ought you not rather to mourn? Let him who has done this to you be removed from among you." 1 Corinthians 5:1-2

It is obvious though that in the Corinthian church there had been some people turning a blind eye to this sexual sin in their church. It is likely that people tried to do something about the situation, and in frustration of the lack of a solution decided to ignore it. Therefore, it is evident that this information was leaking into the community and getting back to Apostle Paul. When confronted with real issues on the difference between godly living and sinful, it becomes common to hear people say things like "Well you know God knows my heart." or "You don't know me!" or the best one being "Only God can judge me!" You can fill in the blank, name the sin. Not everyone is going to have an affair with a stepparent. Often many have things they hide that could easily be taken care of by obeying James' teaching ***"...confess your sins to one to another, and praying for one another that you may be healed"*** (James 5:16a). God does know our hearts, and does judge (Jeremiah 17:10), but He is also perfectly holy and tempered. He is patient, kind, doesn't envy, He is not arrogant, He bears all things, believes all things, hopes all things, and endures all things (1 Corinthians 13: 4, 7).

So when you hear that small voice inside that pleads with you to bring yourself to God and resolve an issue, or when a Christian friend or relative brings a matter to you, don't trust that prideful response and put up your fists. Rather, trust God that in His loving you, He is making a way for you to be whole. The only other option after continuing to disrespect yourself, fellow believers, and God by staying in your sin is to take what I'll call the Kimmy Gibbler rule: ***"Let your foot be seldom found in your neighbor's house, lest he have his fill of you and hate you"*** (Proverbs 25:17). If you cannot think of someone like this, then you may be this person. Don't let this happen. Do not hide in sin. Confess your sins to God, be free, and move forward.

HOLINESS AND SIN

Alex Reiman | Pastor's Academy

"For though absent in body, I am present in spirit; and as if present I have already pronounced judgment on the one who did such a thing. When you are assembled in the name of the Lord Jesus and my spirit is present, with the power of our Lord Jesus, you are to deliver this man to Satan for the destruction of the flesh, so that his spirit may be saved in the day of the Lord" (1 Corinthians 5:3-5).

These verses, if you have never studied them before, are shocking. When we read them, it should send a small shiver down our spine. You may say to yourself "did he really say give him over to Satan?" That is exactly what Paul the writer of 1 Corinthians is saying. He says that there is a man among the Church that is living an unrepentant sin.

Today verses like this leave us with an awkward feeling in our soul. The phrase may pop into your mind; love the sinner and hate the sin, but what do we do when someone we love, loves his or her sin? Is it not our duty to love them since our God is love? Make no mistake that our God is one of great immeasurable love but one attribute of His nature that always is overlooked is His holiness.

God is holy. He is so holy that it is hard for us to wrap our minds around it. He is purer than the whitest snow. He has no evil or wicked part in His whole being. The Bible describes heavenly creatures, who day and night never stop saying, "Holy, holy, holy is the Lord God." He is so holy that men like Isaiah could not help but feel lost and undone in the presences of God.

Our God is one who is always holy all the time and to even fathom His holiness for an instant should make us feel at our very best unclean.

The apostle Peter writes this in response to us who have received the saving power of Jesus Christ and are now new creations in Him. ***"He who called you is holy, you also be holy in all your conduct"*** (1 Peter 1:15). Since God has called us into His eternal family and given us a new life in Jesus, our lives should look different than they did before. Our lives should be one that pursues holiness. We should want to live lives of purity because our heavenly Father is Himself the very essence of purity and holiness. However, when a member of the family or person who says they are in the family is not pursuing holiness we have to confront them in love and say, "your actions not only defile you but also the family name." If they still do no turn from their sin and continue in it, then that is when it is time for them to leave.

During the Civil War, thousands of soldiers were wounded in battle. There were so many men that needed medical attention. The field hospitals were not adequate to perform necessary procedures. Most wounds would become infected and threaten the life of the soldier, so the surgeons did the only thing they could do to save the body from certain death. They amputated the infected part of the body to save the rest of it.

The one who continues in their sin and defiles God's name and His Church is that infection. It is only a matter of time before it will infect the rest of the body of the Church. That is why Paul says to throw that man to Satan for the destruction of his flesh. However, Paul gives us hope that maybe when the man is in his lowest part of his being that there would be nowhere to look but up at God and finally turn from his wicked ways.

1 CORINTHIANS 5: DEVOTION 3

THE BUDDY SYSTEM

Barry Harrison | Pastor's Academy

Do you remember when you were younger and teachers would pair you up with someone else on a field trip so that you each kept an eye on the other and didn't wander off? You know, the "buddy system." Paul illustrates the importance of this concept in 1 Corinthians. Let's look at some similarities of Paul's world and how things are now.

If we spend a little time looking around as we travel about in our daily lives, it is easy to identify potential "idols" that are seemingly everywhere. The newest cars sitting in the showroom, the latest high tech must have gadgets that beg for our attention, and even the promise of escape from daily stress that awaits just inside the party store or pharmacy. Whatever your particular "Golden Calf" may be, the world that surrounds us has it all in plain sight. Not much has changed since the time that Paul wrote 1 Corinthians to the church in Corinth. Corinth was a major Roman city in southern Greece, populated by Romans, Greeks, and Jews. It was a wealthy city that was diverse in religious influences and rich with symbols and tributes to pagan idols. Unbridled sexuality and promiscuity were the order of the day. The feel good culture was on full display in Corinth.

Paul, who at the time of this letter was in the city of Ephesus, continued to be deeply disturbed by the reports of immorality within the church at Corinth. Specifically addressing the church in 1 Corinthians 5:3-5, Paul indicates though he is ***"absent in body"*** he is ***"present in spirit" "through the power of our Lord Jesus."*** Paul is ***"grieved of the Spirit"*** by these reports of pagan (worldly) corruption that have planted seed within the church. He understands that if it is not dealt with and rooted out, it will destroy the church as well as spoil any fruit that has been produced. Paul indicates he has ***"already pronounced judgment on the one who did such a thing."*** He also declares the sentence ***"to deliver this man to Satan for the destruction of the flesh."***

So, wait a second, Paul is calling for one of the men in the church to be handed over to Satan? On the surface, this seems like a very harsh judgment. What authority did Paul have to judge anyone? Isn't that God's place to judge? We find such authority discussed in Mathew 18 regarding dealing with sin amongst believers. Not only was Paul right to judge and act as he was compelled to by scripture. Ok, but handed over to Satan? Matthew 18:17 says if a believer refuses to listen even to the church then treat them as an unbeliever and exclude them from fellowship within the body of Christ.

So what is the purpose of such a sentence, being handed over to Satan for the destruction of the flesh? Yes, we are compelled to keep watch over the integrity of the body of Christ for the continuing sanctification and purifying of the Church. This process exists to protect the Church from unchecked unrepentant sin. In effect Paul is handing this person over to the "ruler of this world" (Satan, 2 Corinthians 4:4) for the opportunity to realize that such behavior leads to spiritual death and that through repentance and the grace of God this person would be restored.

So, like Paul and the church in Corinth, we must see the potential for destructive sin to enter our church by our everyday surroundings. The "idols" we see everyday can find their way into our lives and the church. We must have the courage and love for our brethren to confront sin amongst each other with the purpose of bringing the Church closer to God, and, in the process, strengthening the brethren. Our church leaders bear the biblical responsibility and carry God's authority to protect the church and afford the offender the opportunity to repent and, by God's grace, be restored.

Matthew 18:15 ***"If your brother sins against you go tell him his fault..."*** Sounds like Jesus' version of the "buddy system."

CONFRONTATION

Kyle Wendel | Children and Student Ministries Director

Have you ever had someone sin against you? I am sure we all have had it happen because just like us, everyone sins! Something that is often missed is how to deal with conflict and confrontation biblically. More often than not, we go and tell everyone how someone wronged you. Then it becomes the gossip going around. Instead of telling you how to deal with conflict, I am going to go straight to the Bible.

Matthew 18:15 says, ***"If your brother sins against you, go and tell him his fault, between you and him alone. If he listens to you, you have gained your brother."***

Does scripture tell us to go gossip to anyone when someone wrongs you? Not at all. One of the most important things to do when someone sins against you is to go and talk to that person alone. You should not be making a big scene for all to see, or to create drama. The Bible says first to go to that person and discuss that fault. This needs to be done out of love. Do not go to a person and attack them. We need to confront sin in a loving way as Christ. Christ did not allow sin but did not condemn people. He led the way with true love. When you confront the sin, that person listens, and the conflict is resolved, then you have gained a brother.

Matthew 18:16-17 continues, ***"But if he does not listen, take one or two others along with you, that every charge may be established by the evidence of two or three witnesses. If he refuses to listen to them, tell it to the church. And if he refuses to listen even to the church, let him be to you as a Gentile and tax collector."***

If the person does not repent when you confront them alone, then you need to move onto the next process of Matthew 18, which is to bring in another person or two as witnesses. Again, this is not your opportunity to gossip. Find some godly people that you can trust that will bring godly insight and will not go gossip after. When this conversation about the sin comes again, we hope that the person will now realize they are in the wrong and repent.

If that person still refuses to repent then, we are to bring the matter to the church. Once brought to the church, if the person still decides not to repent, then this process becomes very hard. As God says, we are to let that person go and see them as a Gentile and tax collector. These are not nice titles. This is to let someone go out of the fellowship of the church and thought of as an unbeliever. This is someone who is openly rebellious against the Lord. This process is not supposed to happen quickly. We do not want to confront the person and then an hour later release them from the fellowship of the church. This needs to be done out of love. Even letting the person go is out of love. We pray that the emptiness and loneliness will bring them back to the Father.

My first experience with church discipline was not fun. It hurt. The matter involved friends of mine and was a big situation. In my experience, I was the second witness brought into the story. I did what the Word of God said and handled it according to Matthew 18. In the end, I lost my friendship with this person and a few others. They did not like the way it was handled, even though it was biblical. I stood firm to the Word of God even if that meant I lost friendships. I hope that we become a church that sticks firmly to what the Word of God says.

REMOVE THE LEAVEN

John Carter | Pastor's Academy

How do church Discipline and Holiness connect with each other?

In I Corinthians 5:6-8 we see Paul discussing a topic based on leaven. In a society where everything is prepackaged, this idea may be a little foreign to us. We do not quickly associate leaven with anything relatable in current culture unless you are a baker or someone that makes their bread frequently. (Leaven is like yeast used to make bread rise) In the time this passage was written, it would have been common practice for everyone to know the basic applications of leaven because many of homes made their bread. Let's look at some other passages that use the term leaven and try to use scripture to interpret scripture. In Matthew 16:6 we see Jesus say, ***"Watch and beware of the leaven of the Pharisees and Sadducees."*** At first, the disciples also struggle with making the connection of leaven and it is not until verse 12 that they get it... ***"Then they understood that he did not tell them to beware of the leaven of bread, but of the teaching of the Pharisees and Sadducees."***

Now let's read the passage in I Corinthians 5:6-8 and see if it can make a little more sense to us: ***"Your boasting is not good. Do you not know that a little leaven leavens the whole lump? Cleanse out the old leaven that you may be a new lump, as you really are unleavened. For Christ, our Passover lamb has been sacrificed. Let us therefore celebrate the festival, not with the old leaven, the leaven of malice and evil, but with the unleavened bread of sincerity and truth."***

We have to consider the passages prior and after these verses to get the full context, but I think you can start to see the message pretty clearly. The idea is that leaven (sin/false teachings) is likely to affect the whole congregation. His exhortation is that we are to remove it so that it does not affect the rest of the body. This can apply on several levels. It can be applied to the individual basis and dealing with the sins we allow in our personal lives. Our boastings are not good! It can be applied to the church level in dealing with the proper methods of church discipline. Whether it is used on a micro level or macros level, the same truth holds that we are to recognize the most critical point and logical reason for the removal of sin. ***"For Christ, our Passover lamb, has been sacrificed"*** Hebrews 9:14 says, ***"how much more will the blood of Christ, who through the eternal Spirit offered himself without blemish to God, purify our conscience from dead works to serve the living God."*** It is a denial of Christ's power if we do not deal with the tough issues of discipline and sin as the author of Hebrews says, ***"How much MORE will having Christ purify our conscience..."*** This is a direct correlation to Holiness. Paul gives as the methodology in which we are to deal with these difficult issues. He says to deal with them in sincerity and truth in contrast to malice and evil. Malice means the intention or desire to do evil.

Paul is clear in his message on what we are to do with sin and how we are to approach discipline. The festival that he is talking about, in these verses, is the Passover festival, which is a Jewish celebration of redemption out of slavery. This ties into the subject matter perfectly. The individual's hope and or celebration is knowing that there is redemption from the slavery of sin. The hope for the church in following proper church discipline is the redemption of the disciplined person. When that happens, it is something to celebrate. James 5:19-20 says, ***"My brothers, if anyone among you wanders from the truth and someone brings him back, let him know that whoever brings back***

a sinner from his wandering will save his soul from death and will cover a multitude of sins."

TURN ON THE LIGHTS

Jason Duncan | Pastor's Academy

My wife and I are blessed with three young boys from the ages of 3-7. This means aside from the occasional vacation or grandparent sleep over that we have not had a decent night's sleep in about eight years. I include pregnancy months because nobody ever warns you about that little marriage "gem." One night (as it happens all too often) our youngest wakes up in the middle of the night screaming and crying. As the good father and husband that I am, I immediately jumped right up to attend to his need while allowing my wife to get some much-needed rest (please note sarcasm). As not to wake the two other boys sleeping in the same room and turn this into a real nightmare for myself, I leave the lights off as I enter the room. Now I know the layout of the room because I moved every piece of furniture in there (as I moved my music gear collection out several years ago... *deep sigh, looking heavenward, hands clasped, and repeating with broken voice... my music gear collection*).

Needless to say, at 2:00 am on a "you-name-it" night, with the lights off, I am a little disoriented. I made my way to the edge of his bed being very careful to sweep my feet along the wood floor shooing away toys when it happens again. Embedded into the heel of my foot is none other than the creative gift of Satan himself - a Lego. How could my favorite childhood toy become such a source of evil? This little piece of injection-molded plastic may as well be the tar coated nail sinking into Marv's naked foot from "Home Alone." The pain is unreal, but because I am a Christian and read my James chapter 3 devotion, I keep my mouth on lockdown.

Obviously, if I had turned the lights on, I would have seen the Lego, and thus avoided it! As a Christian, because of the illumination of the Holy Spirit, I can spot sin and identify it when I see it. Bear that illustration in mind as we read Paul's words at the end of 1 Corinthians 5:11-13: ***"But now I am writing to you not to associate with anyone who bears the name of brother if he is guilty of sexual immorality or greed, or is an idolater, reviler, drunkard, or swindler—not even to eat with such a one. For what have I to do with judging outsiders? Is it not those inside the church whom you are to judge? God judges those outside. "Purge the evil person from among you."***

If we have the ability to spot sin by the illumination of the Holy Spirit, then why in the world would we let our brother or sister in Christ step into it? Likewise, if we have spotted an obvious sin in him or her, why would we not make them aware of it and go about the means of correcting it? (Read Matthew 18 in tomorrow's devotion). God gives us His Spirit to live in us; it is a tremendous gift to which we will be sealed with unto the day of redemption. How grievous would it be of us to ignore sin or make light of it? Sin is the very thing that is keeping us separated from fellowship with God at this very moment! Sin is the very thing that assures your death in this life! Sin is the very thing Christ died for on your behalf!

It happens all too often, rather than confront our brother or sister with the issue; we keep our mouths shut to "keep the peace." We redirect our judgment to the unsaved because they are easier targets; we focus our attention on them because by doing so we think we are taking the focus from our "friends" and ourselves. The truth is, however, outsiders are not sealed with the Holy Spirit, which means that they cannot identify the very sins that they are actively engaged in. Without God shining His light on their sin, they will not see it, and without God shining His light on your sin, you would not see yours either.

The direction from Paul is clear: do not judge those who are outside of the faith, rather judge (or hold accountable) those inside the faith, and if they are unwilling to repent, they must be purged from among us. We cannot allow sin to continue unchallenged because it will be sure to lead to destruction. Remember the words of James, ***"Let him know that whoever brings back a sinner from his wandering will save his soul from death and will cover a multitude of sins."***

7

TAKE ONE FOR THE TEAM

Dr. Randy Johnson | Growth Pastor

According to the American Bar Association, there are over one million lawyers in the United States. That means we have more lawyers than doctors. It has been said that Americans are either suing or being sued.

What is the craziest lawsuit you have heard of?

___

___

___

When one of you has a grievance against another, does he dare go to law before the unrighteous instead of the saints? 2 Or do you not know that the saints will judge the world? And if the world is to be judged by you, are you incompetent to try trivial cases? 3 Do you not know that we are to judge angels? How much more, then, matters pertaining to this life! 4 So if you have such cases, why do you lay them before those who have no standing in the church? 5 I say this to your shame. Can it be that there is no one among you wise enough to settle a dispute between the brothers, 6 but brother goes to law against brother, and that before unbelievers? 7 To have lawsuits at all with one another is already a defeat

for you. Why not rather suffer wrong? Why not rather be defrauded? 8 But you yourselves wrong and defraud—even your own brothers!

What are the options when one has a grievance against another?

____

____

____

Why should a believer, who has a grievance against another believer, not take his case outside the church?

____

____

____

"I was never ruined but twice - once when I lost a lawsuit, once when I won one." Voltaire

How could one win a lawsuit and be ruined? ______________

____

____

Why not rather suffer wrong? (verse 7) - What does this mean?

____

____

____

Is it "wrong" to let someone get away with doing "wrong"?

____

____

____

9 Or do you not know that the unrighteous will not inherit the kingdom of God? Do not be deceived: neither the sexually immoral, nor idolaters, nor adulterers, nor men who practice homosexuality, 10 nor thieves, nor the greedy, nor drunkards, nor revilers, nor swindlers will inherit the kingdom of God. 11 And such were some of you. But you were washed, you were sanctified, you were justified in the name of the Lord Jesus Christ and by the Spirit of our God.

Sanctified means "set apart for God". How does verse 11 relate to the rest of the chapter? ____________________________________

____

____

How does verse 11 relate to us today? ____________________

____

____

12 "All things are lawful for me," but not all things are helpful. "All things are lawful for me," but I will not be dominated by anything. 13 "Food is meant for the stomach and the stomach for food"—and God will destroy both one and the other. The body is not meant for sexual immorality, but for the Lord, and the Lord for the body. 14 And God raised the Lord and will also raise us up by his power. 15 Do you not know that your bodies are members of Christ? Shall I then take the members of Christ and make them members of a prostitute? Never! 16 Or do you not know that he who is joined to a prostitute becomes one body with her? For, as it is written, "The two will become one flesh." 17 But he who is joined to the Lord becomes one spirit with him. 18 Flee from sexual immorality. Every other sin a person commits is outside the body, but the sexually immoral person sins

against his own body. 19 Or do you not know that your body is a temple of the Holy Spirit within you, whom you have from God? You are not your own, 20 for you were bought with a price. So glorify God in your body.

What is meant by the distinction between “lawful” and helpful” in verse 12? ______________________________

____

____

How does verse 7 relate to verse 12? ______________________________

____

____

Can you think of other examples conveying the distinction between “lawful” and “helpful”? ______________________________

____

____

Paul moves from the topic of food to sex quite quickly. What is the correlation between these topics? ______________________________

____

____

What do you think of when you see the word “flee” (verse 18)? Can you think of a relevant Bible story (hint: Genesis 39)?

____

____

____

How should we glorify God in your body (verse 20)?

____

____

WEEK 7

"No man is worth his salt who is not ready at all times to risk his well-being, to risk his body, to risk his life, in a great cause."
Theodore Roosevelt

What is your "great cause"?

THE RULES OF THE GAME

Pastor Jayson Combs | Family Pastor

"When one of you has a grievance against another, does he dare go to the Law before the unrighteous instead of the saints. So if you have such cases, why do you lay them before those who have no standing in the church?" (1 Corinthians 6:1 and 4)

My son loves games. Board games, card games, you name it. For better or for worse, he has developed the same competitive spirit as me. Basically, he hates to lose. The other night we were playing an amazing game of UNO when he decided to change the rules. He wanted to start the game with more cards. Then, he wanted to add his own cards to the game with their own specific directives. In summary, he did not want to play by the original rules but wanted to add his own rules when it would work out for his own benefit.

As followers of Christ, we have rules to follow. These rules come from the all-knowing, all-powerful God, who is Truth. He is the one who decides what is right and what is wrong. All truth comes from Him. The Bible is God's truth to us, and it gives us direction on how to live and how not to live. Whether we like it or not, we do not have the ability or the right to change the rules.

In the passages above, Paul gives the people of Corinth some specific truth that was revealed unto him from God. He tells the people of Corinth to stop using the worldly court systems for their grievances, cases, or disputes against other believers.

Why would God, through Paul, give this instruction? It is well known that the church in Corinth was a wreck. The believers were suing one another for their own benefit, and because it felt necessary in the moment. In reality, however, the people of Corinth were killing their own testimony. Rather, Phillipians 2:3-4 says, ***"Do nothing from selfish ambition or conceit, but in humility count others more significant than yourselves. Let each of you look not only to his own interests, but also to the interests of others."***

The truth given by Paul was not only for the people of Corinth but is also truth for our present church. As followers of God's truth, we should be able to work through our issues, to humble ourselves and to look to the interests of others. Using the court means you have gone outside of God's plan, believing your plan works better. Let's remember that the world we live in today no longer follows God's rules. Therefore, why do we think those who do not follow God's direction will give us a better resolution? Who is actually benefitting?

If you are struggling with how to deal with a dispute in the church, I would suggest studying Matthew 18 and Romans 12.

PIG-PEN

Pastor Jayson Combs | Family Pastor

"And such were some of you. But you were washed, you were sanctified, you were justified in the name of the Lord Jesus Christ and by the Spirit of our God" (1 Corinthians 6:11).

There is a character in the Charlie Brown series named Pig-Pen. I am sure you will remember him because he is the boy who is always dirty. No matter what he does or where he goes, a cloud of dust and dirt follows him. On a few occasions in the comic strip, Pig-Pen actually tries to get clean. Yet every time he fails. In fact, at one point he is quoted as saying, I have "reached the point of no return."

As I was studying chapter six of First Corinthians, verse eleven stuck out like a sore thumb. I could not help but think about how Christ has washed me clean. I just had to take some time to thank God for the forgiveness of sins. However, immediately, I was struck with memories of so many sins that I have committed. It is amazing how much of a battle we have with our flesh. Satan is so good at bringing guilt into our lives. He brings up the past so that we will dwell on it. I am so thankful the Lord reminds us repeatedly about the forgiveness of sin.

Revelation 1:5-6 reminds us that the Lord ***"loves us and has freed us from our sins by his blood."*** Through the blood of Jesus, we have been washed from our sins and have freedom! We never have to say that we have "reached the point of no return." Unlike Pig-Pen, we are cleaned! Through Christ, we have been justified. This is the act of being pronounced righteous, or "just if I'd never sinned."

So the next time Satan brings up the sins of your past, remember your justification in Jesus Christ. Remember that you have been washed and that you stand righteous before the Almighty God because of your faith in Christ. Take time to pray today and thank God for that forgiveness.

"For our sake he made him to be sin who knew no sin, so that in him we might become the righteousness of God" (1 Corinthians 5:21).

RUN AWAY (PART 1)

Pastor Jayson Combs | Family Pastor

"Flee from sexual immorality. Every other sin a person commits is outside the body, but the sexually immoral person sins against his own body" (1 Corinthians 6:18).

The Bible says that sexual sin is different from all other sin. John MacArthur puts it like this when he says, "There is a sense in which sexual sin destroys a person like no other, because it is so intimate and entangling, corrupting on the deepest human level."

The church in Corinth was a corrupt church. In verse 13, Paul quotes a common thought from Corinth, ***"Food is meant for the stomach and stomach for the food."*** This is in reference to how the pagan culture of Corinth viewed sex. Just as our bodies need food, our bodies have the urge for sex. Since we have that urge, Paul agrees that we should be able to fulfill it. However, Paul continues with a vital question, saying, ***"Do you not know that your bodies are members of Christ?"*** Paul emphasizes here that God is the creator of sex and it is a good thing, but only under His plan.

With that being said there are two questions I would like to address. 1) What is sexual sin and 2) How do we defend ourselves against it?

The Bible uses two main words to describe sexual sin. First, there is adultery. Adultery is identified as a married person who has sexual relations outside of their marriage. The second word is fornication, which is directed at any person, married or unmarried, who sins sexually with their body.

Ephesians 5:3 says, ***"But sexual immorality and all impurity or covetousness must not even be named among you."*** Other translations say that there should not even be a hint of sexual sin named among us. As I have worked in the youth world for so many years, I have found that many 'church kids' think that only sex outside of marriage is wrong. To them, everything else is fine. When you study the Bible on sexual sin, however, it speaks of much more than just adultery. Jesus even says that if we think about sexual sin in our mind, we are sinning.

1 Thessalonians 4:4 says that we, as followers of Christ, must ***"know how to control his own body in holiness and honor."*** It also tells believers in Christ not to take what is not theirs. If we have a sexual relationship with one who is not our spouse we could be stealing something from a brother or sister in Christ. With teenagers, I ask them what they want their future spouse to be doing in their high school relationships. Then I encourage them to control their own body, as we will look more at tomorrow.

Since sexual sin can be so devastating, we must know what the Bible is talking about when it comes to sexual sin. Paul responded to the church in Corinth by saying we are God's, and we should honor Him with our bodies. This must always be our goal; to honor Him in everything we do. (Part 2 tomorrow)

RUN AWAY (PART 2)

Pastor Jayson Combs | Family Pastor

"Flee from sexual immorality. Every other sin a person commits is outside the body, but the sexually immoral person sins against his own body" (1 Corinthians 6:18).

Yesterday we dealt with the question "What is sexual sin." Today, we will look at how to avoid it. The Bible is very specific when it comes to dealing with the temptation of sin. Ephesians 6:11 says, ***"Put on the whole armor of God, that you may be able to stand against the schemes of the devil."*** James 4:7 says, ***"Submit yourselves therefore to God. Resist the devil, and he will flee from you."*** These verses tell us to stand up against the devil and to resist the devil. When it comes to sexual sin, however, the Bible gives a different command.

I Corinthians 6:18 Flee Fornication.
2 Timothy 2:22 Flee youthful passions.
1 Corinthians 10:14 Flee from idolatry.

The Bible tells us to run away from sexual immorality and to be as far away from it as possible. In these situations, we are not big enough to stand up against it. John MacArthur gives five steps to avoiding sexual sin in his New Testament Commentary. First, he says that to maintain purity, we must avoid a look. Proverbs 6:25 says, ***"Do not let her capture you with her eyes."*** Secondly, avoid flatter. Proverbs 5:3 says, ***"For the Lips of a forbidden woman drip honey and her speech is smoother than oil."*** Next, avoid thoughts. Proverbs 6:25 says, ***"Do not desire her beauty in your heart."*** The fourth point is to avoid rendezvous

(Proverbs 7:7-12). Finally, avoid the house. Proverbs 7:25 says, ***"Her house is the way of Sheol going down to the chambers of death."***

Many times, sexual sins start with just a thought or a glance. We must guard ourselves, however, against our flesh and temptation. For many years, I have taught high school students about sexual sin. I am constantly amazed at the lack of accountability theses students have when it comes to sexual temptation. Whether it is with their phone or computers, many of them have a wide open door that leads to sexual sin. When the Bible tells us to flee fornication, I believe these are the types of things that we must actually be fleeing. Are there things in your life that are opening doors to these temptations? If so, learn to run away. Set up people who can keep you accountable for what you do and what you see.

Sexual sin affects us differently than other sins. Learn to run from these sins that can be so hurtful.

CHEATED

Pastor Jayson Combs | Family Pastor

"To have lawsuits at all with one another is already a defeat for you. Why not rather suffer wrong? Why not rather be defrauded? But you yourselves wrong and defraud—even your own brothers!" (1 Corinthians 6:7-8)

I hate being cheated out of something. You know those guys who always wait until the last minute to merge over on the road so they can cut in front of everyone? You know when you get a bill, and there are those extras fees that were never spoken of? You know when your football team controls the entire football game and the punter fumbles the ball on the very last play? It feels awful not to get what you deserve.

Well, God has convicted me. In 1 Corinthians, God says you do not always have to get what is right. Life is not about getting what we deserve. If it were, we would all be in big trouble. God says the wages of sin is death (Romans 6:23). This means we all deserve death, but it is only because of the grace of Jesus that we have life.

In Corinth, Paul was seeing the church destroy itself because everyone acted as if someone owed him or her something. As we saw yesterday, this behavior was hurting the testimony of the church. In contrast to everything they felt, Paul said it was better to be defrauded than to hurt the church. He said it was better to be wronged than to destroy a relationship with a fellow believer.

This is a constant theme through the Bible that we need to remember today. Jesus says in Matthew 5 that if someone sues you for your shirt, give him or her your coat also. Paul, in Romans

12, says to ***"Bless those who persecute you."*** He does not say to retaliate. Rather, ***"Repay no one evil for evil, but give thought to do what is honorable in the sight of all."*** Verse 19 even says to ***"never avenge yourselves but leave it to the wrath of God."*** Further, Paul writes, ***"if your enemy is hungry feed him."*** Lastly, ***"Do not be overcome by evil, but overcome evil with good."***

I feel completely beat up now. In my egotistical ways, I catch myself acting evil towards people who act evil towards me. I often respond ungraciously and unloving. I pray that we as the church learn to love first, and to see people how Jesus sees them.

1 CORINTHIANS 6: DEVOTION 6

WHO'S THERE?

Pastor Jayson Combs | Family Pastor

"Or do you not know that your body is a temple of the Holy Spirit within you whom you have from God? For you were bought with a price so glorify God in your body" (1 Corinthians 6:19-20).

Do you have someone in your life that changes how you view things? For example, I specifically remember several instances of watching television at my parents' home during my middle and high school years. I would be completely engrossed in the television show, but the moment my father entered the room, I would be quick to change the channel. This was especially true when the material in the show was something my dad would not approve of. In moments like these, my dad literally changed the way I looked at things. Do scenarios like this happen only during the teenage years? Absolutely not, it still happens today!

If you have been reading our 1 Corinthians devotionals, you have come to realize that the church in Corinth had some messed up views. In this chapter alone, Paul deals with two huge issues, suing and sexual sin. Paul wraps up the chapter and further reminds the church they have the Holy Spirit of God living inside of them. Why do you think Christ would have to remind the church of Corinth that the Holy Spirit was with them? I believe it is because He wanted them to remember who was continually present in their lives. He wanted them to remember Him and repent of sinful ways. I do not believe this instruction was just for the church in Corinth. It is still relevant for the church today, which lives their lives without an eternal and biblical perspective.

In Psalms 139, we find the same truth about the Spirit.

Psalms 139:6-12
"Where shall I go from your Spirit?
Or where shall I flee from your presence?
If I ascend to heaven, you are there!
If I make my bed in Sheol, you are there!
If I take the wings of the morning
and dwell in the uttermost parts of the sea,
even there your hand shall lead me,
and your right hand shall hold me.
If I say, 'Surely the darkness shall cover me,
and the light about me be night,'
even the darkness is not dark to you;
the night is bright as the day,
for darkness is as light with you."

The Holy Spirit is with us always; He sees what we do and where we go. There is no hiding or deleting things from the Holy Spirit. Remember that if you know Jesus, the Spirit of God is already inside of you. With this understanding, we should change the way we act, the way we speak, and the way we love.

Verse 20 summarizes this great principle: ***"We are bought with a price so glorify God in your body."*** If you are truly a child of God and the Holy Spirit is inside of you, maybe tonight you will turn off that TV show because you know He is in your presence.

WEEK 7

8

THE BED AND BEYOND

Dr. Randy Johnson | Growth Pastor

To resolve problems in the church, we often need to start at home. There were divisions in the church, and it appears there was a struggle with unity in the home. There was selfishness in the church, and it appears there was a lack of love at home. Sex was a problem in the church, and it appears to have been the battle in the home. Disunity, selfishness, and sex are a formula for disaster.

Now concerning the matters about which you wrote: "It is good for a man not to have sexual relations with a woman." 2 But because of the temptation to sexual immorality, each man should have his own wife and each woman her own husband. 3 The husband should give to his wife her conjugal rights, and likewise the wife to her husband. 4 For the wife does not have authority over her own body, but the husband does. Likewise the husband does not have authority over his own body, but the wife does.5 Do not deprive one another, except perhaps by agreement for a limited time, that you may devote yourselves to prayer; but then come together again, so that Satan may not tempt you because of your lack of self-control.

Do you believe it is easier to love a submissive wife and that it is easier to submit to a loving husband (Ephesians 5)? Who should act first? ____

____

____

From this passage, whose needs are more important?

____

____

____

Sex in the home is a spiritual issue (verse 5). How should a couple approach this? ____

____

____

"You know you're in love when you can't fall asleep because reality is finally better than your dreams." Dr. Seuss

6 Now as a concession, not a command, I say this. 7 I wish that all were as I myself am. But each has his own gift from God, one of one kind and one of another.

How can being single be a gift? What are some of the advantages of being a single Christian? ____

____

____

8 To the unmarried and the widows I say that it is good for them to remain single as I am. 9 But if they cannot exercise self-control, they should marry. For it is better to marry than to burn with passion.

What is implied by "self-control" in verse 9?

____

____

____

10 To the married I give this charge (not I, but the Lord): the wife should not separate from her husband 11 (but if she does, she should remain unmarried or else be reconciled to her husband), and the husband should not divorce his wife.

What is the difference between divorce and being separate from each other? ____

____

____

If a spouse separates, is that scriptural grounds for divorce?

____

____

____

"There is no more lovely, friendly, and charming relationship, communion or company than a good marriage." Martin Luther

12 To the rest I say (I, not the Lord) that if any brother has a wife who is an unbeliever, and she consents to live with him, he should not divorce her. 13 If any woman has a husband who is an unbeliever, and he consents to live with her, she should not divorce him. 14 For the unbelieving husband is made holy because of his wife, and the unbelieving wife is made holy because of her husband. Otherwise your children would be unclean, but as it is, they are holy. 15 But if the unbelieving partner separates, let it be so. In such cases

the brother or sister is not enslaved. God has called you to peace. 16 For how do you know, wife, whether you will save your husband? Or how do you know, husband, whether you will save your wife?

What principles does Paul give for Christians who are married to an unbeliever? ____

____

____

If you are a Christian and your spouse isn't, is that scriptural grounds for divorce? ____

____

____

If the unbelieving spouse leaves, is there a scriptural ground for divorce? ____

____

____

What other legitimate reason for divorce is recorded in scripture (Hint: Matthew 19:9)? ____

____

____

What goal is presented in verse 16? ____

____

____

"Our culture says that feelings of love are the basis for actions of love. And of course that can be true. But it is truer to say that actions of love can lead consistently to feelings of love." Timothy Keller

17 Only let each person lead the life that the Lord has assigned to him, and to which God has called him. This is my rule in all the churches. 18 Was anyone at the time of his call already circumcised? Let him not seek to remove the marks of circumcision. Was anyone at the time of his call uncircumcised? Let him not seek circumcision. 19 For neither circumcision counts for anything nor uncircumcision, but keeping the commandments of God. 20 Each one should remain in the condition in which he was called. 21 Were you a bondservant when called? Do not be concerned about it. (But if you can gain your freedom, avail yourself of the opportunity.) 22 For he who was called in the Lord as a bondservant is a freedman of the Lord. Likewise he who was free when called is a bondservant of Christ. 23 You were bought with a price; do not become bondservants of men.24 So, brothers, in whatever condition each was called, there let him remain with God.

What general guideline does Paul give (verses 17, 20, and 24)?

___

___

___

What was their social status in the world's eyes?

___

___

___

What was their status in God's eyes (verse 22)?

___

___

___

25 Now concerning the betrothed, I have no command from the Lord, but I give my judgment as one who by the Lord's mercy is trustworthy. 26 I think that in view of the present distress it is good for a person to remain as he is. 27 Are you bound to a wife? Do not seek to be free. Are you free from a wife? Do not seek a wife. 28 But if you do marry, you have not sinned, and if a betrothed woman marries, she has not sinned. Yet those who marry will have worldly troubles, and I would spare you that.29 This is what I mean, brothers: the appointed time has grown very short. From now on, let those who have wives live as though they had none, 30 and those who mourn as though they were not mourning, and those who rejoice as though they were not rejoicing, and those who buy as though they had no goods, 31 and those who deal with the world as though they had no dealings with it. For the present form of this world is passing away.

How has your marital status (single or married) helped you to serve more effectively? ________________________________

____

____

Where has your marital status challenged or limited your ministry? ____

____

____

For the present form of this world is passing away reminds us that times are changing, and that time is limited. Look what we are told to do in Colossians 3:12-14, ***"Put on then, as God's chosen ones, holy and beloved, compassionate hearts, kindness, humility, meekness, and patience, bearing with one another and, if one has a complaint against another,***

forgiving each other; as the Lord has forgiven you, so you also must forgive. And above all these put on love, which binds everything together in perfect harmony."

How would Colossians 3 affect our relationships?

____

____

____

32 I want you to be free from anxieties. The unmarried man is anxious about the things of the Lord, how to please the Lord.33 But the married man is anxious about worldly things, how to please his wife, 34 and his interests are divided. And the unmarried or betrothed woman is anxious about the things of the Lord, how to be holy in body and spirit. But the married woman is anxious about worldly things, how to please her husband. 35 I say this for your own benefit, not to lay any restraint upon you, but to promote good order and to secure your undivided devotion to the Lord.

Are verses 32-33 always true, or general observations?

____

____

____

How might a single person be too anxious about the world and a married individual find it easier to be anxious about the things of the Lord because they are married? ____________________

____

____

36 If anyone thinks that he is not behaving properly toward his betrothed, if his passions are strong, and it has to be, let him do as he wishes: let them marry—it is no sin. 37 But whoever is firmly established in his heart, being under no necessity but having his desire under control, and has determined this in his heart, to keep her as his betrothed, he will do well. 38 So then he who marries his betrothed does well, and he who refrains from marriage will do even better.

This passage isn't saying that passion is all you need in choosing a marriage partner. What traits would you suggest in looking for a lifelong partner? ______________________________

____

____

39 A wife is bound to her husband as long as he lives. But if her husband dies, she is free to be married to whom she wishes, only in the Lord. 40 Yet in my judgment she is happier if she remains as she is. And I think that I too have the Spirit of God.

May a widowed individual remarry? ____________________

____

____

In what practical way can you use your marital status (single, married, divorced, remarried, widowed) to your advantage this week? ____

____

____

WEEK 8

"[Spiritual friendship] is eagerly helping one another know, serve, love, and resemble God in deeper and deeper ways." Timothy Keller

1 CORINTHIANS 7: DEVOTION 1

SEX AND LOVE

Pastor Jeff England | Counseling Pastor

The Corinthian Church had issues. Many issues. It was a church of misfits. They communicated with the Apostle Paul looking for answers and guidance as they struggled to become a Christ-centered body. Paul patiently and lovingly teaches these baby Christians through his two letters that are now a part of our New Testament.

In the first nine verses of 1 Corinthians Chapter 7, we read about Paul discussing marriage, intimacy, and fornication. He bluntly discusses the fact that you do not have to marry, but if you choose to marry, you must be committed to this one person. He warns of the dangers of sexual immorality amongst the married and the unmarried. The Corinthian Church was struggling with purity. Perhaps you or someone you know has a similar struggle.

Our world has changed in so many ways over the years. I find myself reminding and encouraging parents to protect their children from exposure to sinful sexuality. It is such a monumental challenge with today's television content, the Internet, and lust filled images practically everywhere. The use of pornography is destroying marriages at an alarming rate and creating a country where many kids are growing up thinking they have to be sexual to be accepted.

Paul teaches there is only one Godly avenue for sexual fulfillment, marriage. This fulfillment should be wonderful! Two people, committed to each other as one, sharing the incredible God-given joy of loving each other for their lifetimes. Oh how man has altered the Creator's design. Sexual intimacy has become a scapegoat for struggling marriages and adulterous behavior. God blessed us with sex as not only a fun way to procreate but as an expression of our love and commitment to our spouse. However, we have often very selfishly turned it into a reward for desired behavior. Others use it as a tool to be given or withheld as a means of expressing their present feelings about their spouse. I remind couples often that their sexual intimacy is not the key to a healthy marriage but more of a barometer for the condition of their marriage. Generally, when a man loves his wife like Christ loves the Church and a woman respects her husband's God-given authority (See Ephesians Chapter 5), physical intimacy is mutually cherished. A marriage filled with resentment and insecurity most often creates an unhealthy or non-existent sex life that can lead to a great deal of other problems. Paul taught us the importance of the marital covenant. He encouraged us to submit our bodies to our spouses and not to deprive each other of sexual intimacy. Husband and wife need to be able to share their thoughts and feelings about sex openly with each other.

It is my hope for you and your spouse that you will continue to build your marriage into what God designed it to be. Remember, a marriage is a marathon not a series of sprints. No matter the health of your marriage at this time, it can improve with your commitment to walk intimately with Christ. This walk will give you the strength to love your spouse unconditionally.

Growth Moment – Read the "Love Chapter," 1 Corinthians 13. In verses 4-7, Paul gives us 15 qualities of true Biblical love. Sit down with your spouse and in a spirit of humility openly discuss your thoughts on how well each of you is displaying these qualities in your relationship. Go a step further and discuss whether these same qualities are being demonstrated any differently in the bedroom.

MARRIAGE VOWS

Pastor Jeff England | Counseling Pastor

The Corinthian Church had a long list of struggles. One of their biggest weaknesses was honoring their marriage vows. Divorce was becoming a major spiritual and social issue. Sound familiar? Yes, our divorce rate today in the US shows one of every two marriages is failing. That number climbs as high as three of four failing on second and third marriages. Children of divorced parents are up to four times more likely to divorce as adults than children from parents that stay married (Reported by US Census Bureau 2009). Please remember God is always bigger than statistics!

Paul's emphasis in our passage today is Jesus' command back in Mark 10 Verse 9. ***"What God has joined together let not man put asunder."*** I believe Scripture is clear that marriage is a sacred covenant meant to truly last until death. Both Jesus and Paul discuss situations in a marriage where divorce may occur but even in the darkest times, it is worth fighting for your marriage. If you are divorced, please know there is no condemnation here. Whatever happened in the past does not mean God will not bless your future if you are living your life for Jesus. God loves and forgives all of His children.

As I write this devotion, I am receiving texts from a person whose spouse has committed adultery. This individual feels defeated and wants to give up. I am encouraging perseverance and that the spouse be given the time to process the consequences of sin. The pain is great, and the individual admits to a lack of personal obedience to God for years that contributed to an environment ripe for temptation. I am hopeful a living example of patience and forgiveness may reflect Christ in a way that the spouse has a heart change. We must not doubt God's power to heal our pain and broken trust.

When I was a kid, I broke my left arm twice in the same spot. I had not gone to the doctor after the first break. When it healed the second time, the doctor showed us my x-ray that revealed a huge calcium buildup at the exact spot where the breaks occurred. "You will never break that arm there again," he proclaimed. "It is stronger than any other spot in your body." This incident reminds me of broken people in relationships that have endured sinful choices. When God heals hearts, they can be stronger than ever before. Healing a broken marriage is not about the counselor. It is about two people committing their lives to God and each becoming the person He desires. When we are intimately walking with God, no problem is impossible to conquer.

Some of you have married someone who is not walking with Christ at this time. It does no one any good to regret the marriage and your partner's lack of relationship with Jesus is not grounds for divorce. Too many times, I have heard someone justify divorce with the words, "We should have never married." Paul gives us very practical advice in our passage today. He says in verses 12 and 13 of Chapter 7 that if your unsaved spouse wants to stay in the marriage, you need to stay in the marriage. He goes on to say in verse 16 that by staying, there is an opportunity to possibly persuade your spouse to become a believer. I know many couples that are not walking together as God planned and I know the Christian partner often struggles. These individuals and their spouses need our love, support, and prayers. Reach out, encourage, and become an active prayer partner to these hurting brothers and sisters.

WEEK 8

Growth Moment – Do you know a couple that is not walking together as God intended? Make a point this week to pray for them that the believer perseveres and the non-believer becomes saved. Build your relationship with both by extending offers to get together and hang out.

PRIORITIES

Pastor Jeff England | Counseling Pastor

In today's passage, it appears many of the Corinthians were struggling to understand what was truly important after they accepted Christ. Paul writes to give them clarity on what should be priorities for new Christians. I am always amazed and excited at the zeal of many new believers. When one has truly committed their heart to Jesus, you can literally watch them break free of the shackles that have kept them in bondage for so long. I will never forget observing the changes in a man around our church many years ago who had been a miserable, chronic alcoholic. When he came to know Jesus, he became (and remains today) a joyous, excited man who could not get enough of God's Word. He studied Scripture with such passion that the changes in him were dramatic. Another part of my memory of him was that the only Bible he owned at the time of his salvation was an extremely large, coffee table type of family Bible which he carried everywhere and held with great enthusiasm. It was heart-warming and humorous to see him coming to church with a huge smile and a Bible nearly the size of a watermelon.

I imagine many of the Corinthians had this same enthusiasm as they committed their lives to Christ. However, some must have believed that they had to make extreme changes and lost the concept of being content in the position they were in when called into the family of God. Some Jewish men actually thought they should no longer be circumcised as Christians, and they endured a procedure to reverse their circumcision. Ouch! Paul stresses to them in verses 17-19 that issues like circumcision were not a priority. He later, in verses 21-24, uses the example of slaves to point out we must be content in the situation in which we are. He wanted the Corinthians to stop worrying about status and position changes and focus on what was really important which was living God's way. He makes it clear in verse 19 when he states, "Circumcision does not matter and uncircumcision does not matter, but keeping God's commandments does."

It remains true today. God has called each of us to our own position in life. We need to strive for excellence in whatever that calling is. Are you an attorney? Be a Godly attorney. A plumber? Be a Godly plumber. A stay at home mom? You get the picture. What is important is not your position, but how you carry yourself in Christ every day in whatever your role you are given opportunities to reflect Him.

I have met many over the years who have told me God has called them into ministry. This often means they believe they should quit their jobs, possibly get some training, and start earning a living working for a church or Christian organization. Some of these same people became discouraged and frustrated because their plans did not work out as they had expected and they did not receive a paying job in ministry. This situation can create a lot of mixed emotions and upset families because frequently so much time and resources were invested in the change.

God calls people to serve in many different ways and from all walks of life. He does call people to take positions that do involve employment but the vast majorities who are called to serve maintain their current positions but live their lives differently. They take their free time and invest it into any one of a host of ministries around their home or church. Opportunities abound in serving individuals including widows, shut-ins, and the less fortunate. Your church usually needs workers in their nurseries, youth ministry, and outreach activities. Be faithful in the role and opportunity God provides and let Him direct you if He should want you hired into full-time ministry. Your willingness and faithfulness are all God needs to do something incredible in your life.

Growth Moment. Are you serving in your Church or community? I know your life is full but find an opportunity to reflect Christ by serving and stick to it. Let's see how God uses you!

ETERNAL MINDSET

John Sanchez | Deacon of Operations

Paul, addressing the concerns of the Corinthian church, submits his godly opinion on the question of marriage. He speaks to them during a time of immense persecution. Focusing on their spiritual well-being and preservation during this "present distress," he offers up what seems to be practical spiritual advice.

"Are you bound to a wife? Do not seek to be free. Are you free from a wife? Do not seek a wife. But if you do marry, you have not sinned, and if a betrothed woman marries, she has not sinned" (Verses 27-28).

Paul is speaking to the questions that occupy the minds of the Corinthian believers, but he expands the narrative to address the real heart of the matter. He redirects their focus from the question of marriage to the priorities of their lives.

"This is what I mean, brothers: the appointed time has grown very short. From now on, let those who have wives live as though they had none, and those who mourn as though they were not mourning, and those who rejoice as though they were not rejoicing, and those who buy as though they had no goods, and those who deal with the world as though they had no dealings with it. For the present form of this world is passing away" (Verses 29-31).

Now do not be confused. Paul is not discouraging or bashing marriage by any means. He is speaking to a body of believers who have become entangled in the worldliness of the culture surrounding them. The culture, rather than God's Word, governed their mindset. The fact is, under Roman law and culture there existed several different kinds of marriage arrangements. Also, at the crossroads of this pagan culture was Corinth, a corrupt and ungodly city whose influence had seeped into the church - creating an unholy mess.

So Paul encourages the Corinthian believers to direct their affairs here on earth, with an eternal mindset:

"Let those who have wives, as if they had none" (Verse 29). Paul by no means is instructing husbands to cast off their marital responsibility, but rather to lead with the mindset and example of one who's primary focus in life is to please Christ and to understand his return is imminent (the appointed time has grown short).

"Those who mourn as though they were not mourning, and those who rejoice as if they were not, and those who buy as though they had no goods" (Verse 30). Paul is calling the Corinthians to task for becoming quite content and comfortable in the prosperous worldly culture that surrounded them. Their joys and sorrows were dictated by the varying degree of their worldly "Status."

"And those who deal with the world as though they had no dealing with it" (Verse 31). As Jesus said, we are in this world but not of this world. Paul admonishes the believers to responsibly conduct their affairs on earth with the mindset of a sojourner. As such, this world is not our home. We are not setting up permanent residence; we are just passing through.

Let's not hastily judge our Corinthian brethren as we read this epistle. Rather, let's take this opportunity to examine our lives to determine if we have let the values of our 21st-century American culture govern our hearts.

Are we conforming ourselves to the prevailing culture around us?
Or are we allowing God's Word to shape lives?
Are you living as if Christ will return today?

ABSURD OFFER

John Sanchez | Deacon of Operations

"For the present form of this world is passing away." (1 Corinthians 7:31b)

Can I interest you in some Dutch Tulips? They are beautiful flowers; no doubt, you will enjoy them. Yes, you say? Wonderful, I have just the one for you – a rare gem. Will cost you a tidy $2,500. Wait that is too much you say? Ok, I have a more common variety. It's a steal at $1,200.

Now before you choke on the absurdity of this offer, would you doubt me if I told you it actually happened? Even more, would you believe me if I told you there were hundreds (if not thousands) of people who paid these ridiculous amounts of money for these Dutch Tulip bulbs? Furthermore, those who did buy them did not even plant them! They would display them in their bulb state, considering them too valuable to plant. It was the Dutch Tulip Bulb mania of 1637. It started and crashed all in the same year.

I always find stories like this fascinating, and hard to believe. What drives people to deem some things worthless and other things so valuable? This is what Paul highlights to the Corinthian believers in 1 Corinthians 7:31.

The ancient Greek city of Corinth was one of the largest and prominent cities of its time. Having two major ports and roads converging from all parts of the known world, it was the center of activity in its corner of the Roman world. Traders, merchants, artisans, professionals, citizens, and slaves from around the world made their way through Corinth. It was a cosmopolitan city in every sense of the word.

This was the environment surrounding the young Corinthian church started by Paul. It experienced significant prosperity under Roman rule. This prosperity threatened to cloud the Corinthian believer's understanding of whose kingdom they served. Their lifestyles indicated they were placing their faith and truth in the permanence of 'this present world'.

Self-examination is no easy task. I find myself challenged to examine my inner priorities when I study God's word. If I am honest, there are times I look deep inside and question my resolve, my devotion, and my authenticity. I, like Paul, sometimes find myself torn between two extremes. On the one hand cleaving to what I consider important, and on the other realizing the vanity of it all in light of God's truth.

It is a healthy struggle. What would make it unhealthy is if the struggle did not exist. The human soul lulled into apathy and complacency is oblivious. It takes a strong (violent?) jolt out of our slumber to awaken us to the truth.
The present form of this world is passing away.

Are you vesting in the eternal or the temporal?

A PIECE OF PEACE

John Sanchez | Deacon of Operations

"I want you to be free from anxieties" (1 Corinthians 7:32a).

Ever experience anxiety? Worry? Fear? Sometimes emotions hit us in "bundles," making it hard for us to figure out what it is we are feeling. One thing is certain; it is not a peaceful feeling.

Paul, addressing the Corinthian believers' concerns on marriage, makes his intentions clear. His primary concern was their spiritual health - their complete devotion to Christ. Anything distracting or competing for this devotion should be purposefully examined.

We see this in verse 35, ***"I say this for your own benefit, not to lay any restraint upon you, but to promote good order and to secure your undivided devotion to the Lord."***

The last part of that verse jumps out at me, ***"undivided devotion to the Lord."*** If you are like me, life throws a lot at you. Our responsibilities span across family, work, personal relationships, ministry, you fill in the blank. Sometimes I find myself allowing the urgent things to crowd out the important things - my relationship and devotion to the Lord.

It is the classic Mary and Martha conundrum (read about it in Luke 10:38-42).
Martha was busy tending to the 'urgent' while Mary sat at the feet of Jesus tending to what was 'important'.

Paul's concern for the young Corinthian church shows in his

appeal to their priorities. Their anxiety, like ours, is directly related to what they consider important.

Responsibilities are real, we all have them, and we do not run from them. However, acknowledging our dependence and need for Christ to lead and direct us keeps all the pieces of the puzzle in its proper focus.

How about you? What's consuming your mind and thoughts to the point of anxiety today? Have you submitted it to the Lordship of Christ, or are you letting it weigh you down?

Remember Jesus' word:
"Come to me, all who labor and are heavy laden, and I will give you rest." Matthew 11:28

That kind of love from an amazing Savior is worth all of my devotion.

How about you?

WEEK 8

9

SMART OR HEART?

Dr. Randy Johnson | Growth Pastor

---

1 Corinthians is going to evaluate two words through the next several chapters: Freedom and rights. Entitlement creeps in as the struggle goes between "me first" and "you first."

How do you handle disagreements – do you get loud and have to win, seek compromise, give in quickly, or close down?

____

____

____

Now concerning food offered to idols: we know that "all of us possess knowledge." This "knowledge" puffs up, but love builds up. 2 If anyone imagines that he knows something, he does not yet know as he ought to know. 3 But if anyone loves God, he is known by God.

Why does Paul contrast knowledge with love?

____

____

____

How can knowledge puff up? ________________________

____

____

How can love build up? ____

____

____

Which is most important: know about God, know God, or be known by God? ____

____

____

"The only true wisdom is in knowing you know nothing." Socrates

4 Therefore, as to the eating of food offered to idols, we know that "an idol has no real existence," and that "there is no God but one." 5 For although there may be so-called gods in heaven or on earth—as indeed there are many "gods" and many "lords"— 6 yet for us there is one God, the Father, from whom are all things and for whom we exist, and one Lord, Jesus Christ, through whom are all things and through whom we exist.

What theological foundation does Paul lay down here?

____

____

____

How could the "sides" be classified as overconfidence and too sensitive of a conscience? ______________________________________

____

____

Do one of the sides have to be wrong? Does Paul scorn the strong or the weak brother? ______________________________

____

____

What item or activity have you given up for the sake of others even though you feel you have freedom? ______________________________

____

____

"People talk about the middle of the road as though it were unacceptable. Actually, all human problems, excepting morals, come into the gray areas. Things are not all black and white. There have to be compromises. The middle of the road is all of the usable surface. The extremes, right and left, are in the gutters." Dwight D. Eisenhower

7 However, not all possess this knowledge. But some, through former association with idols, eat food as really offered to an idol, and their conscience, being weak, is defiled. 8 Food will not commend us to God. We are no worse off if we do not eat, and no better off if we do. 9 But take care that this right of yours does not somehow become a stumbling block to the weak. 10 For if anyone sees you who have knowledge eating in an idol's temple, will he not be encouraged, if his conscience is weak, to eat food offered to idols? 11 And so by your knowledge this weak person is destroyed, the brother for whom Christ died. 12 Thus, sinning against your brothers and wounding their conscience when it is weak, you sin against Christ. 13 Therefore, if food makes my brother stumble, I will never eat meat, lest I make my brother stumble.

What does it mean to be a "weaker brother"?

What did it feel like when you stood alone on a topic?

Could something be a sin for one person and not for another?

What are some issues where some Christians think they have freedom while other Christians think one is "crossing the line"?

"Free will carried many a soul to hell, but never a soul to heaven."
Charles Spurgeon

IS THE BARGAIN WORTH IT?

Carole Combs | Women's Ministry

"If food makes my brother stumble, I will never eat meat, lest I make my brother stumble." 1 Corinthians 8:13

The Apostle Paul addressed the believers in Corinth concerning the meat that was offered to the pagan idols. Some believers were purchasing the meat at such a bargain price from the pagan temples because it was much cheaper than the local meat market. However, there was confusion among the church. Some were wondering if it was appropriate for those that were getting the bargain meat to eat of it. They knew that idol worship was wrong, and many thought that eating that meat would make them participants in idol worship.

In this small chapter, Paul addresses several issues concerning the heart and actions of a believer. He wanted them to consider if that bargain meat was worth causing others to stumble in their faith.

Many of you will remember the time when there was not an expiration date on food items. After the dates were out on items, many items in my refrigerator that became "expired" according to my kids. They would refuse to use salad dressing or even have a drink of milk from a carton that was one day after the expiration date. Finally, after coming over for dinner and eating at Mom and Dad's house became a time for date checking, I threw everything away. I did not want my family or a guest in my home to stumble at my dinner table. I wanted our time together to be focused on what matters rather than what I thought was all right.

WEEK 9

"Let us not pass judgment on one another any longer, but rather decide never to put a stumbling block or hindrance in the way of a brother" (Romans 14:13).

What are you holding on to that is causing others to stumble? Is it worth it?

BIG HEAD OR BIG HEART?

Carole Combs | Women's Ministry

You have to admit that when you were nineteen years old, you knew everything. You wondered how your parents were not so smart and that you had exceeded their intelligence. I was just finishing my first year at the university, and I was getting married. Newly married, we had a beautiful spacious apartment, a nice car, and good jobs. We were living the American Dream. Then reality hit! You know the bills, the arguments, the stresses, and the difficulties of life. What dream I was living in suddenly turned into a nightmare in my mind. Remember, I knew everything, so why was it not going "my" way?

I am so thankful that God has a heart of compassion. He gently moves and surrounds us with circumstances and situations that draw us close to Him. 1 Corinthians 8:1b says that ***"knowledge puffs up, but love builds up."*** My know-it-all self was consumed with my ways, with my wants, and expectations. God showed me that the only real dream in this world we live in is His way, or if you may, His dream for you! We can be so focused on our plan that it will not matter who we run over in the process. Most often that plan of yours that you raced to was a dead end. When you arrived, you still had that feeling of emptiness and loneliness.

On the contrary to what the world teaches, knowledge will give you a big head and turn your focus inward, but love builds up and turns your focus outward. Do not get me wrong; I love to learn. I am continually a student of all the things that surround me. Most importantly, I am a student of the things of God. I love God and His Word and His Church. It is only through loving these when you will truly understand what real love is.

WEEK 9

"For God so loved...that He gave..." (John 3:16)

"Love the Lord with all your heart, soul and mind...and your neighbor as yourself." (Matthew 22:37-39)

Are you more concerned about your agenda or God's agenda?

Do you have a big head or a big heart?

FAKE GODS

Carole Combs | Women's Ministry

...'"An idol has no real existence,' and that 'there is no God but one'. For although there may be so-called gods in heaven or on earth-as indeed there are many 'gods' and many 'lords' - yet for us there is one God, the Father, from whom all things, and for whom we exist." 1 Corinthians 8:4-6

If I had not put the scripture reference next to the words above you would just assume that they were words written by me. Paul, in his letter to the church at Corinth, made it very clear to the believers that any god or lord over and around them is fake. These same words I would say to you.

There is no genuine, authentic deity in them. They are man's imaginable idea of God. Often they were a lucrative opportunity for a person or group of people. What is sad to me is that this scripture is still relevant today. The world has allowed so many gods and lords to take the place of the one true God. For example, who is Mother Nature? A replacement for the one true God that makes His sunrise on the evil and on the good and sends rain on the just and on the unjust. (Matthew 5:45) The Stork? Easter Bunny? Father Time? Santa Clause? I know I am picking on your childhood memories and mine as well. Can you see where the world wants us to put our focus on these characters or idols so that our focus is removed from the one true God?

Idols are not just characters with names. Idols can be anything or anyone that precedes or takes the place of God. When we give all our time and energy, when we give our passion and possessions to the idols of this world, we are worshipping them. God gets the leftovers or nothing at all from us. God is put in the closet for safekeeping. We treat God as if he is a vending machine expecting Him to dispense at our demand. We may seek Him only when the gods of this world are not meeting or fulfilling our expectations. ***"Thou shalt have no other gods before me"*** (Exodus 20:3).

What fake God have you placed before the one true God?

How is it working for you?

WOE IS ME

Carole Combs | Women's Ministry

"So whoever know the right thing to do and fails to do it, for him it is sin" (James 4:17).

Ouch! How many times have you and I knowingly done things that we thought we should not do? The Spirit of God even spoke to our hearts and mind to make the right choice but we chose our way, and it was seldom by accident. The Bible calls this sin. Ouch again!

In 1 Corinthians 8:7, Paul teaches that a person can defile their conscience. Puritan Richard Sibbs wrote in the seventeenth century that, "the conscience is at the heart of what distinguishes the human creation. People, unlike animals, can contemplate their own actions and make moral self-evaluations. The conscience leads you to do what you believe is right and restrains you from what you believe is wrong."

The conscience is not the voice of God. It is a part of us that God gave to you and me to filter our actions and thoughts. It is by the standard we know.

So what is your standard? What do you use to measure right and wrong in your life? If your standard measures up better than your neighbor, your siblings, your spouse, you may think that you are doing good in the eyes of God. What if you measured yourself to God? When Isaiah saw God in the book of Isaiah 6:5, he said, ***"Woe is me! I am a sinful man..."*** Since Isaiah had seen God and all His righteousness, he measured his life against God and saw how sinful he was.

It is so easy to compare and learn our standards of living from those around us. I am so thankful that God has given us His living Word that we might put the right data in our consciences. We have His Word to filter our thoughts and actions. Take time today to delete those things in your mind and in your heart that are defiling you. I do not want to say “Ouch” every day, and I am sure you do not either. Your words need to be saturated with the words of God. Make your choices and actions honor God all the time.

What is your conscience telling you?

1 CORINTHIANS 8: DEVOTION 5

TO EAT OR NOT TO EAT, THAT IS THE QUESTION

Carole Combs | Women's Ministry

One, two, three pray after me and POOF! Your relationship with God is all set. This world we live in has mixed up and messed up how we can have a relationship with God. Paul deals with this very subject. ***"Food will NOT commend us to God. We are no worse off if we do not eat, and no better off if we do."*** 1 Corinthians 8:8

When the teens go to camp, they have had food eating contests. They are not your typical pie, jello, or marshmallow eating contests. The contests have included pig brains, rotten eggs, and blended up worms to name just a few. My daughter would come home talking about these games, only to make me queasy hearing about them. Yes, they would win a prize for succeeding to stomach these not so normal food items. Paul was clarifying that it was not what you ate or what you did not eat that had any merit to a closer relationship with God.

So how do we draw closer to God? It is an action on our part. God always does his part.

"...How can we know the way? Jesus said to him, 'I am the way, and the truth, and the life. No one comes to the Father except through me'" (John 14:5, 6). ***"When I am lifted up from the earth, I will draw all people to myself"*** (John 12:32).

Our only way to the Father in heaven is through Jesus. Jesus knew there would be confusion, heartaches, and troubles in this world. There are times that I go to my "feel good" food, which includes ice cream and chocolate, of course. It is temporary, I know. However, what are you relying on that you do to have a relationship with

God? Jesus said that He has ***"come to give us life, but not just life, but an abundant life also"*** (John 10:10b). We have the ability in this world we live in to live an abundant life! It is a life rich in God's mercy and grace! It is a life surrounded by God's goodness!

To eat or not to eat should never be the question.

To trust God and follow Him is the answer.

ORDER ME UP A BIG MAC

Carole Combs | Women's Ministry

It has been my choice since 2014 never to eat McDonalds' foods. The choice was merely for better eating habits. However, before the year 2014 was to end, Jim and I drove to Selma, Alabama to visit our dear friends who are in their eighties. Jim went fishing early in the morning that next day after we arrived with Joe. Meryl and I made plans the night before to go to breakfast together in the morning. Being in a small southern town, I was looking forward to enjoying some great southern cooking for breakfast. As we drove through the town, Meryl pulls into McDonalds. I was screaming in my mind, "Oh, no, I didn't plan on coming here again." Did I say anything to Meryl? Absolutely not! I ate my egg McMuffin and enjoyed our time together.

Paul says that we can sin against our brothers...thus sinning against God (1 Corinthians 8:11, 12). Not hurting Meryl's feelings was more important to me than a food choice I had made. We will answer to God for our actions, but we will also answer to God how we have treated others.

"For I was hungry and you have me food, I was thirsty and you gave me drink, I was a stranger and you welcomed me. I was naked and you clothed me, I was sick and you visited me, and I was in prison and you came to me. Then the righteous will answer him, saying, 'Lord when did we see you hungry and feed you, or thirsty and give you drink? And when did we see you a stranger and welcome you, or naked and clothe you. And when did we see you sick or in prison and visit you?' And the King will answer them, 'Truly, I say to you, as you did it to one of the least of these my brothers, you did it to me'" (Matthew 25:35-40).

What a sobering verse to realize that our actions toward others speak volumes to whom we serve. Is it the God of self or the God of the universe? I have not had McDonalds since that time, but if I am going to sin against my brother, order me up a Big Mac!

10

SPRINT, MARATHON OR OBSTACLE COURSE

Dr. Randy Johnson | Growth Pastor

In the middle of his letter, Paul takes the time to give his credentials. The Corinthians were taking great pride in their freedom in Christ. It was hurting others and clearly a distraction from what the Gospel was really about.

Am I not free? Am I not an apostle? Have I not seen Jesus our Lord? Are not you my workmanship in the Lord? 2 If to others I am not an apostle, at least I am to you, for you are the seal of my apostleship in the Lord.

A characteristic of being an apostle was being an eyewitness of the resurrection of Jesus Christ and having been commissioned to proclaim the gospel to all nations. Did Paul qualify (Acts 9:1-9; 22:6-16; 26:12-18)? ________________________________

____

____

If we used a wax seal in place of our signature today, what would be your "mark"? ___________________________________

____

____

3 This is my defense to those who would examine me. 4 Do we not have the right to eat and drink? 5 Do we not have the right to take along a believing wife, as do the other apostles and the brothers of the Lord and Cephas? 6 Or is it only Barnabas and I who have no right to refrain from working for a living? 7 Who serves as a soldier at his own expense? Who plants a vineyard without eating any of its fruit? Or who tends a flock without getting some of the milk?

Why do you think Paul didn't feel free using some of his rights?

____

____

____

Are there practices today that Christians should be careful in expressing or exhibiting their freedom? ______________

____

____

8 Do I say these things on human authority? Does not the Law say the same? 9 For it is written in the Law of Moses, "You shall not muzzle an ox when it treads out the grain." Is it for oxen that God is concerned? 10 Does he not certainly speak for our sake? It was written for our sake, because the plowman should plow in hope and the thresher thresh in hope of sharing in the crop. 11 If we have sown spiritual things among you, is it too much if we reap material things from you? 12 If others share this rightful claim on you, do not we even more?

Paul refers to the Old Testament by referring to the Law of Moses. Priests did not go into the "workforce." They focused on worshipping God and helping others do the same.

Could this have applied to Paul? ______________________________

____

____

Does this apply today? ______________________________

____

____

Nevertheless, we have not made use of this right, but we endure anything rather than put an obstacle in the way of the gospel of Christ. 13 Do you not know that those who are employed in the temple service get their food from the temple, and those who serve at the altar share in the sacrificial offerings? 14 In the same way, the Lord commanded that those who proclaim the gospel should get their living by the gospel.

What are the strengths and weaknesses of Paul not receiving full support as a missionary? ______________________________

____

____

15 But I have made no use of any of these rights, nor am I writing these things to secure any such provision. For I would rather die than have anyone deprive me of my ground for boasting. 16 For if I preach the gospel, that gives me no ground for boasting. For necessity is laid upon me. Woe to me if I do not preach the gospel! 17 For if I do this of my own will, I have a reward, but if not of my own will, I am still entrusted with a stewardship. 18 What then is my reward? That in my preaching I may present the gospel free of charge, so as not to make full use of my right in the gospel.

What does Paul mean when he says, For necessity is laid upon me (verse 16)? ______________________________

____

____

Can this phrase apply to us today? ______________________________

____

____

19 For though I am free from all, I have made myself a servant to all, that I might win more of them. 20 To the Jews I became as a Jew, in order to win Jews. To those under the law I became as one under the law (though not being myself under the law) that I might win those under the law. 21 To those outside the law I became as one outside the law (not being outside the law of God but under the law of Christ) that I might win those outside the law. 22 To the weak I became weak, that I might win the weak. I have become all things to all people, that by all means I might save some. 23 I do it all for the sake of the gospel, that I may share with them in its blessings.

Paul said, I have become all things to all people (verse 22). What changes do we (and have we already) need to make in order to reach more (or even different) people? ______________________________

____

____

24 Do you not know that in a race all the runners run, but only one receives the prize? So run that you may obtain it. 25 Every athlete exercises self-control in all things. They do it to receive a perishable wreath, but we an imperishable. 26 So I do not run aimlessly; I do not box as one beating the air.

27 But I discipline my body and keep it under control, lest after preaching to others I myself should be disqualified.

What points is Paul making by comparing the Christian life to a race? ____

____

____

"The New Testament says nothing of Apostles who retired and took it easy." Billy Graham

1 CORINTHIANS 9: DEVOTION 1

PASTORAL CARE

Pastor Trevor Cole | Communications Pastor

Let me just start today's study by emphasizing the fact that if I had a choice, I would skip right over this part of the chapter. However, it is part of chapter 9, and I have been asked to write six devotions for chapter 9. We would come up quite short if I skipped over one-third of the chapter because it made me uncomfortable. So here we are...

I would like to do a quick review of 1 Corinthians, so we know where we have come from and where we are headed. Throughout much of this book, Paul has been answering all kinds of questions these church people had been asking. In chapter 8, he introduced the truth of Christian liberty: that we have the right to do certain things because, through Christ, we have been freed from the law. He also explained that our Christian liberty must be controlled by our concern and love for our fellow believers. In other words, there are certain things that we can do that we should not do because of how it will impact those around us. Paul uses all of chapter 9 and some of the next to teach this idea through the example of his own life. Today, let's take a look at verses 1-11.

1 Am I not free? Am I not an apostle? Have I not seen Jesus our Lord? Are not you my workmanship in the Lord? 2 If to others I am not an apostle, at least I am to you, for you are the seal of my apostleship in the Lord.
3 This is my defense to those who would examine me. 4 Do we not have the right to eat and drink? 5 Do we not have the right to take along a believing wife, as do the other apostles and the brothers of the Lord and Cephas? 6 Or is it only Barnabas and I who have no right to refrain from working for a living? 7 Who serves as a soldier at his own expense?

Who plants a vineyard without eating any of its fruit? Or who tends a flock without getting some of the milk?
8 Do I say these things on human authority? Does not the Law say the same? 9 For it is written in the Law of Moses, "You shall not muzzle an ox when it treads out the grain." Is it for oxen that God is concerned? 10 Does he not certainly speak for our sake? It was written for our sake, because the plowman should plow in hope and the thresher thresh in hope of sharing in the crop. 11 If we have sown spiritual things among you, is it too much if we reap material things from you?

Did I already mention that if it were my choice, I would have skipped right over these verses? Paul spends 11 verses emphasizing his right to be supported by the church. He gives all kinds of reasons: Other pastors are supported by their churches (v. 6). Soldiers, farmers and shepherds get gain from what they oversee (v.7-9). You reap what you sow (v.11).

The most painful part about teaching on this is that so many pastors throughout the world are taking advantage of verses like these. There will always be those types of people, those who take advantage of God's Word and abuse it for their own personal gain. Sometimes it is a "pastor" who does not truly want to serve God but serves the almighty dollar. It is not just pastors that misuse God's Word like this though; people do it all the time as well. They manipulate God's Word in a way that fits their argument and disregard it when it does not. However, we cannot avoid the truth of the Bible because we are uncomfortable with those who misuse it. God has called us to financially provide for those who care for our churches, and I hope that we do not take that responsibility lightly.

MY RIGHTS

Pastor Trevor Cole | Communications Pastor

"I deserve." "Get mine." "It is my right." These phrases have become commonplace, not just in the world around us, but in our lives as well. In the verses we looked at yesterday, Paul emphasized his right to be supported financially by the church.

I have been married for 12 years now. They have been 12 of the best years of my life. Despite having the best wife ever, I've still found myself expecting more at times. I have had some moments where I felt like Paul, except on a much more selfish and immature level. You know those classic stupid guy thoughts like "I put my dishes in the dishwasher, I deserve to just sit on the couch the rest of the night now," or even better, "I made the bed once this week and now you have the audacity to ask me to take out the trash?"

Take a moment to examine yourself and remember a recent moment where you had a similar thought about your rights. Read 1 Corinthians 9:12. Remember, Paul has spent most of this chapter reminding the church just how much sacrifice he put in for their lives and how it is his right to be supported by them.

Let's take a closer look at verses 12.

12 If others share this rightful claim on you, do not we even more? Nevertheless, we have not made use of this right, but we endure anything rather than put an obstacle in the way of the gospel of Christ.

In those moments of excessive self-worth, we rarely take into consideration how our "rights" affect the people around us. One of the most disruptive, dare I say, destructive forces in the church today takes place when we misuse the freedom or the rights we have been given by God. Throughout the Bible, God emphasizes the importance of helping and supporting the people around us. 1 Thessalonians 5:11 says, ***"Therefore encourage one another and build one another up, just as you are doing."*** I often find myself focusing on what I am allowed to do instead of focusing on what I should do for those around me.

Paul set himself up as an example to follow. He showed us how he had every right to be supported by the church at Corinth, yet Paul laid down that right for something he knew was far more important: "the gospel of Christ." He knew that these young believers in a relatively young church might have a difficult time supporting him, so he laid his right down for the greater good. When you find yourself demanding what you deserve, ask yourself "is my right what's most important here or do I need to lay down my right to help build someone up?"

1 CORINTHIANS 9: DEVOTION 3

BY ALL MEANS

Pastor Trevor Cole | Communications Pastor

Before we look at anything else Paul writes in this section we need to establish why he did what he did and why we should follow his example. We find his reasoning at the end of verse 22: ***"that by all means I might save some."*** What exactly was he trying to save them from? He may not state it explicitly in this verse but Romans 5:9, another of Paul's letters, reads ***"Since, therefore, we have now been justified by his blood, much more shall we be saved by him from the wrath of God."*** That is exactly what Paul and we are trying to rescue people from, the wrath of God.

Maybe it is because, as Americans, we have so much. Maybe it is just because we do not want to be reminded of God's justice. Whatever the reason may be, we often avoid the fact that the Holy God, who created this earth, must pour out His wrath on those who do not put their faith in the saving work of Jesus. Many people emphasize the help that Jesus can give psychologically, the power to overcome hate, fear, loneliness, and so on. Those things are wonderful, and He does help us to overcome those issues, but the best and most important part of the gospel is that we do not have to experience God's almighty wrath. Do you believe that?

It is entirely possible that we do not share the message of Jesus because we do not believe, deep down, that God's wrath will reign down on those who reject His truth. Our lives have become so busy and so filled with an excess of doing that we take little time to remind ourselves that our lives are short, and people need the truth of Jesus. Take some time today and simply think on the wrath of God that will come. Allow it to impact your view of this world just as it did Paul's.

Once you have allowed the truth and power of God's wrath to sink into your heart and mind, then read the following verses.

1 Corinthians 9:19-23 - ***For though I am free from all, I have made myself a servant to all, that I might win more of them. 20 To the Jews I became as a Jew, in order to win Jews. To those under the law I became as one under the law (though not being myself under the law) that I might win those under the law. 21 To those outside the law I became as one outside the law (not being outside the law of God but under the law of Christ) that I might win those outside the law. 22 To the weak I became weak, that I might win the weak. I have become all things to all people, that by all means I might save some. 23 I do it all for the sake of the gospel, that I may share with them in its blessings.***

Now that we understand Paul's reason, his heart, we can truly understand what it means to be all things to all men. We have freedom in Christ to put aside the petty differences that can alienate us from society and more specifically, from those who do not follow Jesus. We must also remember to examine ourselves regularly before God to make sure that we are not becoming too much like the world that they no longer realize that there is something different about us. This task is not an easy one, but I challenge you to see what God can do through you when you ask yourself this question often: "Am I doing everything I can to reach those around me while remaining true to the God who saved me from His wrath?" Can you say like Paul "that by all means I might save some"?

1 CORINTHIANS 9: DEVOTION 4

RUN WITH PURPOSE

Pastor Trevor Cole | Communications Pastor

I have never loved running. Plenty of people I know have asked me "isn't it on your bucket list to run a marathon?" Nope, not even a little bit. Don't get me wrong; I am a pretty competitive person. I'll bust out the occasional 2-5 mile run just to see what I can do, but 26.2 miles? Yeah, I'll pass on that.

Even though I would not consider myself an avid runner, I think we can all understand the point Paul makes in 1 Corinthians 9:24: ***"Do you not know that in a race all the runners run, but only one receives the prize? So run that you may obtain it."*** There are so many things grasping for our attention on a daily basis with many of them being very worthwhile, valuable pursuits. A successful career, physical fitness, financial security, a happy marriage, who would criticize such pursuits? In and of themselves these goals are benign, but when we allow them to control our every decision, we have left the course of the most important race we must run.

Let's just take a moment and focus on one area that almost everyone desires, a happy marriage. We can all agree that a happy marriage is a good thing and that God has the power to give us just that. The problem arises when we make a good marriage our goal. We believe that a happy marriage will help everything else fall into place. When that happens, we are no longer running in the right race. Our life's goal should be to follow Jesus with everything we have and to share the message of His forgiveness and freedom.

If in my marriage all I am trying to do is make my partner happy and vice versa, we may end up with a "good" marriage by most standards. We stay faithful to one another, enjoy going to dinner and on vacations with one another, and everyone around us thinks "they've got it pretty good." A happy marriage may be a wonderful thing, but it should never be our ultimate goal. Our marriages would be much better off if husband and wife kept eternity in mind. We must remember that God did not bring us together simply for our enjoyment and happiness but so that we could serve Him better. A couple dedicated to giving their all to God instead of just to each other has enormous power.

This idea of keeping eternity in mind applies to any other pursuit in this world as well. Career, fitness, and finances can all be good things if we remember why God has given us those opportunities and abilities: for His glory and to reach others with His good news. A great runner of any kind keeps the end in mind. That is what we must do; focus on what is ahead. It is not easy to live with eternity in mind every day of our lives, but we must give everything we have to focus on the end of our race.

1 CORINTHIANS 9: DEVOTION 5

NOT PERFECT... YET

Pastor Trevor Cole | Communications Pastor

---

1 Corinthians 9:25 – ***"Every athlete exercises self-control in all things. They do it to receive a perishable wreath, but we an imperishable."***

Matthew 5:6 – ***"Blessed are those who hunger and thirst for righteousness, for they shall be satisfied."***

Have you ever failed at something? Have you ever given your all toward something and still come up short? It hurts doesn't it? Trying to live for God sometimes feels that way. We know the sacrifice that Jesus made to give us forgiveness and we long to live for Him in return, but it often feels like we fail Him all the time. For many years I've asked God to make me the man He wants me to be: To lead people to follow Him, to live a holy life, to lead my family His way, to be a loving, kind, and strong husband and so on. I wish I could tell you that I am always all of those things, but I am not.

In 1 Corinthians 9:25 Paul talks about this imperishable wreath or crown: Every athlete exercises self-control in all things. They do it to receive a perishable wreath, but we an imperishable. Yesterday we learned about staying on course and keeping eternity in mind as we run the race that God has for us. Today I want to encourage you with the promise that God has made for those who run the race well. Paul reminds us that those who win races here on earth receive a crown that will eventually be meaningless but that believers run their race for one that is imperishable, but what is the crown he is talking about? The word Paul uses here can be found in other parts of the Bible but the most similar use can be found in 2 Timothy 4:7-8: ***"I have fought the good fight,***

I have finished the race, I have kept the faith. 8 Henceforth there is laid up for me the crown of righteousness..." This crown of righteousness that is promised to those who keep the faith is what makes us fit for heaven. Here on earth we are not perfect. We do the best we can with God's help, but we still make mistakes; we fail Him. I find it so encouraging to know that there will come a day when I no longer falter in this race we run.

It is important and encouraging to remember that this world we live in is not our final home. We are just racing through it, and we must keep our eye on the prize or we will run off course. I'm going to date myself here, but Steven Curtis Chapman wrote a song that never ceases to give me hope; it is called "Not Home Yet." If you have a moment, give it a listen, but let me leave you with these words from the song: "I know there'll be a moment, I know there'll be a place, where we will see our Savior and fall in His embrace. So let us not grow weary or to content to stay, because we are not home yet." We may not be perfect yet, but when we reach our final home, we will be the best version of ourselves that God always had planned for us.

GOALS

Pastor Trevor Cole | Communications Pastor

1 Corinthians 9:26-27 - ***"So I do not run aimlessly; I do not box as one beating the air. 27 But I discipline my body and keep it under control, lest after preaching to others I myself should be disqualified."***

I have already told you that I am no marathon runner but I would not call myself a fighter either. Apart from my younger brother, I have never been in a fistfight in my life. Regardless of not being a fighter, I can get the picture Paul paints when he talks about keeping his body under control. We know that he is a goal setter because he does not want to run "aimlessly." Anyone who has ever trained for anything can relate to that concept.

I remember a few years ago when I realized I had put on a few extra pounds since my college days. I knew I needed to take care of the body God has so graciously given me, and I was sick of feeling as if I was going to die every time I simply jogged down the basketball court. So off I went to get "back in shape." It did not take me long to realize that I needed some goals, so I started writing everything down. Distances and times for runs, weights used, pushups done, and all that. It is funny that when it comes to fitness we know what it takes to get better and move forward. If we are really serious, we do not just want to get by with our training we want to do everything we can to get the best results. If I just go out for a jog every day and do not have anything to compare one day with the next, how will I know if I have grown at all? I won't and I will end up stuck in a rut going nowhere.

God wants us to have the same attitude about goals for our spiritual life. I would encourage you to regularly examine yourself and ask God for some spiritual goals. That can be something as simple as reading a certain book of the Bible for a month or spending a certain amount of time in prayer for a season. We do not want these goals to be a checklist that makes us feel more spiritual; they are to help us grow closer to God.

I would also encourage you, do not try to do it all on your own. Hebrews 3:13 – ***"But exhort one another every day, as long as it is called 'today,' that none of you may be hardened by the deceitfulness of sin."*** Find someone that is almost a spiritual workout partner. Someone you respect that you can be open and honest with about the spiritual goals you want to set. God made us social people and that is no different when it comes to spiritual growth.

11

LESSON LEARNED

Dr. Randy Johnson | Growth Pastor

We can learn from positive role models and positive life experiences from the past. Paul points out that we can also learn from bad experiences and poor role models. Basically, we are told to flee sin and follow the Savior. However, it is not always that clear, so he gives some guidelines for those gray areas.

For I do not want you to be unaware, brothers, that our fathers were all under the cloud, and all passed through the sea, 2 and all were baptized into Moses in the cloud and in the sea, 3 and all ate the same spiritual food, 4 and all drank the same spiritual drink. For they drank from the spiritual Rock that followed them, and the Rock was Christ. 5 Nevertheless, with most of them God was not pleased, for they were overthrown in the wilderness.

Twice Moses and the Israelites experience water flowing from a rock (Exodus 17; Numbers 20). What does Paul mean in saying the Rock was Christ? ____________________________________

____

____

What differences take place between Exodus 17 and Numbers 20? Why? ____

____

____

6 Now these things took place as examples for us, that we might not desire evil as they did. 7 Do not be idolaters as some of them were; as it is written, "The people sat down to eat and drink and rose up to play." 8 We must not indulge in sexual immorality as some of them did, and twenty-three thousand fell in a single day. 9 We must not put Christ to the test, as some of them did and were destroyed by serpents, 10 nor grumble, as some of them did and were destroyed by the Destroyer. 11 Now these things happened to them as an example, but they were written down for our instruction, on whom the end of the ages has come. 12 Therefore let anyone who thinks that he stands take heed lest he fall. 13 No temptation has overtaken you that is not common to man. God is faithful, and he will not let you be tempted beyond your ability, but with the temptation he will also provide the way of escape, that you may be able to endure it.

List the sins pointed out here:

Verse 7 – ____
Verse 8 – ____
Verse 9 – ____
Verse 10 – ____

The word "example" is used twice here (verses 6 and 11). What needs to be done for someone to learn from a bad example?

____

____

"He that gives good advice, builds with one hand; he that gives good counsel and example, builds with both; but he that gives good admonition and bad example, builds with one hand and pulls down with the other."
Francis Bacon

What promises does verse 13 offer? ___________________________

____

____

"I always say God doesn't need me, but I need Him in my life to survive in this world and over temptation. That's Who keeps me humble every time."
Albert Pujols (professional baseball player)

Temptation is the devil looking through the keyhole. Yielding is opening the door and inviting him in.
Billy Sunday (former evangelist and professional baseball player)

How do we know temptation is not sin? _________________________

____

____

14 Therefore, my beloved, flee from idolatry. 15 I speak as to sensible people; judge for yourselves what I say. 16 The cup of blessing that we bless, is it not a participation in the blood of Christ? The bread that we break, is it not a participation in the body of Christ? 17 Because there is one bread, we who are many are one body, for we all partake of the one bread. 18 Consider the people of Israel: are not those who eat the sacrifices participants in the altar? 19 What do I imply then? That food offered to idols is anything, or that an idol is anything? 20 No, I imply that what pagans

sacrifice they offer to demons and not to God. I do not want you to be participants with demons. 21 You cannot drink the cup of the Lord and the cup of demons. You cannot partake of the table of the Lord and the table of demons. 22 Shall we provoke the Lord to jealousy? Are we stronger than he?

Underline the items we are told to "flee" and circle what we are to "pursue".

1 Corinthians 6:18: ***"Flee from sexual immorality. Every other sin a person commits is outside the body, but the sexually immoral person sins against his own body."***

1 Corinthians 10:14: ***"Therefore, my beloved, flee from idolatry."***

1 Timothy 6:10-11: ***"For the love of money is a root of all kinds of evils. It is through this craving that some have wandered away from the faith and pierced themselves with many pangs. But as for you, O man of God, flee these things. Pursue righteousness, godliness, faith, love, steadfastness, gentleness."***

2 Timothy 2:22: ***"So flee youthful passions and pursue righteousness, faith, love, and peace, along with those who call on the Lord from a pure heart."***

What is Paul referring to when he references the cup, the bread, and the table of the Lord (verse 16 and 21)? Why does he refer to these? ____

____

____

What idols are in the world today? ______________________

____

____

God is often referred to as a jealous God (Exodus 20:5; 34:14; Deuteronomy 4:24; 5:9; 6:15; 29:20; 32:16,21; Joshua 24:19; 1 Kings 14:22; Psalm 79:5; Ezekiel 5:13; 16:42; 23:25; 36:5; 38:19; 39:25; Joel 2:18; Nahum 1:2; Zephaniah 1:18; 3:8; Zechariah 1:14; 8:2; and James 4:5). What is meant by it?

____

____

____

Deuteronomy 4:24: ***"For the Lord your God is a consuming fire, a jealous God."***

Nahum 1:2: ***"The Lord is a jealous and avenging God; the Lord is avenging and wrathful; the Lord takes vengeance on his adversaries and keeps wrath for his enemies."***

23 "All things are lawful," but not all things are helpful. "All things are lawful," but not all things build up. 24 Let no one seek his own good, but the good of his neighbor. 25 Eat whatever is sold in the meat market without raising any question on the ground of conscience. 26 For "the earth is the Lord's, and the fullness thereof." 27 If one of the unbelievers invites you to dinner and you are disposed to go, eat whatever is set before you without raising any question on the ground of conscience. 28 But if someone says to you, "This has been offered in sacrifice," then do not eat it, for the sake of the one who informed you, and for the sake of conscience— 29 I do not mean your conscience, but his. For why should my liberty be determined by someone

else's conscience? 30 If I partake with thankfulness, why am I denounced because of that for which I give thanks?

Just because I can do something doesn't mean I should. What guidelines or principle could be applied from verses 23-24?

____

____

____

What is the distinction between tolerating differences and condoning wrong behavior? ____________________

____

____

31 So, whether you eat or drink, or whatever you do, do all to the glory of God. 32 Give no offense to Jews or to Greeks or to the church of God, 33 just as I try to please everyone in everything I do, not seeking my own advantage, but that of many, that they may be saved.

Why does Paul try to please everyone (verse 33)?

____

____

____

Which verse is more relevant to your life right now?

____

____

____

Verse 13 - ***No temptation has overtaken you that is not common to man. God is faithful, and he will not let you be tempted beyond your ability, but with the temptation he***

will also provide the way of escape, that you may be able to endure it.

Verse 31 - ***So, whether you eat or drink, or whatever you do, do all to the glory of God***

"It is not great men who change the world, but weak men in the hands of a great God." Brother Yun (known as "The Heavenly Man")

"Give me 100 preachers who fear nothing but sin and desire nothing but God; such alone will shake the gates of hell." John Wesley

GUILTY UNTIL PROVEN INNOCENT

Pastor Tommy Youngquist | Children's Pastor

Breaking News River Church We are all tempted! Some of you are probably rolling your eyes at me right now, but it is true. Why do we always feel guilty for being tempted? If you are like me, I feel guilt and shame when a thought of sin comes into my mind, and I am tempted to act upon the thought. Here is some more news though. Do you know that being tempted is NOT sin? Jesus was tempted and was without sin! Sin does not occur until the temptation is ACTED upon.

Fighting temptation is hard, whether it is something small like that delicious dessert when trying to lose weight or something huge like believing the whispers heard in the dark that God could not possibly love us and that we have been too sinful. Despite how you view it, we can all agree that defeating temptation is difficult. Here is one of my favorite verses in the Bible:

"No temptation has overtaken you that is not common to man. God is faithful, and he will not let you be tempted beyond your ability, but with the temptation he will also provide the way of escape, that you may be able to endure it." 1 Corinthians 10:13

Paul killed it here! These words are so encouraging to me (someone who, in the past, has said that enduring temptation is impossible). Our God knows we will be tempted, and God Himself will provide an escape plan. Be encouraged River Church! God has provided a way of escape when we think all is lost. Even if you are constantly giving into temptation, the change can happen!

The Former New York Yankees catcher, Yogi Berra once said,

"It ain't over 'till it's over." Now Yogi is no theologian, but he unknowingly expressed one of the greatest principles in the Christian life. It matters little to have the lead at the beginning; what matters is how you finish. Victory is won at the finish line, not at the starting blocks. Moreover, the Christian life is not a 100-yard dash; it is a marathon that requires endurance and a lifetime commitment to keep running with the intent of finishing strong! The cliché, "It ain't over 'till it's over" serves as a reminder to you and me that no matter how you started, life is not over, and you can finish strong!

You are not guilty of sin until YOU make the CHOICE to do it! Quit saying, "This is too hard," "It's impossible not to sin," or "I cannot do it." All excuses! The best things in life are the things we have to work for – the things that do not come easy. God has made a way for us to escape the temptation. The question is... Are you going to look for that way and work for the better choice?

Tomorrow, we are going to look at a practical plan that Jesus Himself laid out for us on how to defeat temptation. I hope you come back and read it. Remember River Church:

"In this world you will have trouble. But be encouraged! I have won the battle over the world." – Jesus (John 16:33 NIRV)

JESUS PRACTICAL PLAN: HOW TO DEAFEAT TEMPATION

Pastor Tommy Youngquist | Children's Pastor

Yesterday we talked about the difference between temptation and sin. Temptation, in and of itself, is not sin until acted upon. Jesus Himself was tempted by Satan and did not sin. 1 Corinthians 10:13 says, ***"No temptation has overtaken you that is not common to man. God is faithful, and he will not let you be tempted beyond your ability, but with the temptation he will also provide the way of escape, that you may be able to endure it."***

That's right! God has made an escape plan. In Matthew 4, Jesus provides a three-step, practical plan on how to defeat temptation and He uses Himself as the example.

"Then Jesus was led up by the Spirit into the wilderness to be tempted by the devil. And after fasting forty days and forty nights, he was hungry. And the tempter came and said to him, 'If you are the Son of God, command these stones to become loaves of bread.' But he answered, 'It is written, Man shall not live by bread alone, but by every word that comes from the mouth of God.' Then the devil took him to the holy city and set him on the pinnacle of the temple and said to him, 'If you are the Son of God, throw yourself down, for it is written, He will command his angels concerning you and on their hands they will bear you up, lest you strike your foot against a stone.' Jesus said to him, 'Again it is written, you shall not put the Lord your God to the test.' Again, the devil took him to a very high mountain and showed him all the kingdoms of the world and their glory. And he said to them, 'All these I will give you, if you will fall down and worship me.' Then Jesus said to him, 'Be gone, Satan! For

it is written, 'You shall worship the Lord your God and him only shall you serve.' Then the devil left him, and behold, angels came and were ministering to him." (Matthew 4:1-11)

1. Temptation comes when we seem weak and defenseless, SO BE ALERT! Jesus was hungry, and Satan used His circumstance to increase the temptation. Know when you a susceptible and be vigilant. (vs. 1 and 2; 2 Corinthians 12:10)
2. The Scriptures are our weapons against temptation, SO ARM YOURSELF! Every time Jesus was tempted, He replied with, "It is written." He knew the Scriptures. We need to arm ourselves with Scripture. Temptation is a mental battle. (vs 4-10; Ephesians 6:17; James 1:25)
3. God is faithful to protect us and provide for us SO THAT WE CAN ENDURE! God made the devil leave and had the angels re-affirm Jesus He chose rightly. He will do that for us, so endure. (v 11; John 14:27; Matthew 6:30)

If we give up and give in, temptation leads to sin (James 1:2-15). However, if we are saved, the Holy Spirit will lead and remind us whose we are, so call on Him (John 14:23-24). God is faithful to protect and provide. There is always an escape plan. We must be faithful and take it!

COMMIT OR QUIT

Pastor Tommy Youngquist | Children's Pastor

When I got married to Ashley, I said yes to fully giving myself to her. She did the same in return. There is no going back to the old, single life. She and I cannot have one foot in married life and one foot in single life. I cannot give half of my heart to her when she gives all of her heart to me. For the relationship to work we have to give up our old way of living and 100% devote ourselves to each other.

The same is true of our relationship with Jesus. When we give our lives to Jesus, He does not become part of our lives; He is our life! That is the message the apostle Paul sends to the church in Corinth in 1 Corinthians 10:14-22. They were eating and drinking the Lord's Supper, then continuing to offer sacrifices or eat at pagan temples. Instead of committing to following Jesus, church members were keeping their options open by continuing to worship at the pagan temple. Paul urges them to stop straddling the fence.

We give Jesus either all or nothing. There is no in-between. Jesus Himself said,

"No one can serve two masters, for either you will hate the one and love the other, or you will be devoted to the one and despise the other. You cannot serve God and money." (Matthew 6:24)

River Church, we cannot chase sin and pursue Jesus at the same time. To pursue one, we must turn our backs on the other. It is a daily struggle (of which we have an escape plan). Every morning when our feet hit the ground, we have a choice to make: Am I going to chase after sin today or am I going to pursue Jesus? Jesus laid down His life for us. He did not hold back from us. Let's not hold anything back from Him.

Reflect on the last three days:

- What one thing are you most tempted by right now?
- Jesus was hungry, so Satan tempted Him with food. When you are tempted, replace those thoughts with 10 minutes of Jesus, the Bread of Life (John 6:35).
- Are you trying to follow Jesus with one foot in sin?
- What is one thing you need to let go of to live fully devoted to Jesus? What step can you take to let it go?

Asking for help to defeat the temptation you face is not always easy. Giving up something from the old life can be hard. You are not the only one trying to give up something that has a stronghold in your life. The staff at the River Church would love to help you. Trust me; we need your help just as much as your need ours. Your church family is here to help you because we understand everyone needs help. Please, email or call us. Set a meeting with one of the pastors. Our job exists to help people. You are important to us. Thanks for reading these past three days. My prayer for you is that you live wholly committed to Jesus as He was to you.

DOES IT CAUSE YOU TO GROW?

Matt Hatton | Student Ministries Director

As followers of Jesus, we are commanded to do everything to the glory of God! In 1 Corinthians 10:31 God's Word directs us, ***"So, whether you eat or drink, or whatever you do, do all to the glory of God."*** This command seems elementary at first glance; however, the way we live proves otherwise. Many areas in the Christian life make it hard to "do all to the glory of God." One of those areas is addressed here in 1 Corinthians 10. One of those areas is the controversial topic of Christian "freedom!" What am I supposed to do about the things that are not specifically addressed in the Bible? Are they right? Are they wrong? This church or pastor says it is right while this other church or pastor says it is wrong. What should I do?

If there is no definitive answer to the question of what is right or wrong because our answer is based upon the one who is answering the question, then we may need to ask some new questions when it comes to the area of Christian freedom. In verse 23 Paul writes, ***"All things are lawful, but not all things are helpful. All things are lawful, but not all things build up."*** When Paul says "All Things," he is referring to all things that are not covered in the Bible as being permissible. What do we do when nothing is written down?

Instead of asking, "am I allowed to do this," ask if it is "beneficial or edifying," Is what I'm doing, having a drink, smoking, watching a certain movie, wearing certain types of clothes, talking a certain way, or going to the Lion's game, going to be beneficial or edifying? Does my activity/behavior cause spiritual advance or growth in my own life? Does it help me to grow and others be drawn to Christ?

(Note: You may have another issue altogether if you enjoy going to a Lion's game just to watch them lose.)

Does whatever you freely choose to do cause you to stumble in any way? Have you been led to sin because of the movie you were watching or because of the people you were hanging out with? Maybe it has not torn you down or caused you to sin, but maybe it has not caused spiritual advancement either. Does said behavior/activity cause you to grow? Do you love Jesus more because of it? Do you seek and want to know more about God and His kingdom as a result? ALL things are lawful, but not always helpful.

MY FREEDOM AND OTHERS

Matt Hatton | Student Ministries Director

When seeking to do "all things" in expressing our Christian freedoms, it is very important that whatever it is that we are doing does not cause us to sin in any way and at the same time creates spiritual growth and advancement of the Gospel in our own lives. The next standard that Paul writes of is found in verses 24-30, ***"Let no one seek his own good, but the good of his neighbor. Eat whatever is sold in the meat market without raising any question on the ground of conscience. For 'the earth is the Lord's, and the fullness thereof.' If one of the unbelievers invites you to dinner and you are disposed to go, eat whatever is set before you without raising any question on the ground of conscience. But if someone says to you, 'This has been offered in sacrifice,' then do not eat it, for the sake of the one who informed you, and for the sake of conscience— I do not mean your conscience, but his. For why should my liberty be determined by someone else's conscience? If I partake with thankfulness, why am I denounced because of that for which I give thanks?"*** Does what you are doing affect those around you?

Does an unbeliever turn even more away from God and want nothing to do with it because of something that you said, did, or even allowed to happen? Have you offended an unbeliever or even another believer with your Christian "freedoms?"
When you are acting upon your Christian freedoms, does it cause your brothers or sisters in Christ to sin? Does it make them uncomfortable in the slightest? If so, then we should not act upon those certain freedoms. There should be no excuse or loopholes that we try to work our way through and around. "Well it's their

fault they were looking at me and has nothing to do with what I'm wearing" or "they're the one who should be putting up safeguards for themselves, I shouldn't have to for them." If you find yourself saying or thinking that sort of thing, then you are without a doubt not being edifying or God honoring with your Christian freedom.

The Bible says in Philippians 2:3-4, ***"Do nothing from selfish ambition or conceit, but in humility count others more significant than yourselves. Let each of you look not only to his own interests, but also to the interests of others."*** It is important to make sure we do not lead others into sin, but what we do and say should also cause them to grow! Often our problem is not that we are unaware of right from wrong or beneficial from hurtful, but the problem is selfishness from selflessness. We know when we should or should not do something; instead, we often do what we want no matter what because that is all we care about! I will end with this, 1 Corinthians 10:33, ***"not seeking my own advantage, but that of many, that they may be saved."*** Are you looking out for your own good or the good of others with your freedom?

ALL TO THE GLORY OF GOD

Matt Hatton | Student Ministries Director

The reason for using our Christian freedom carefully and selflessly is none other than to glorify God. Paul writes in 1 Corinthians 10:31 ***"so, whether you eat or drink, or whatever you do, do all to the glory of God."*** When Paul is talking about eating and drinking, he is referring to the food and drink offered to idols while at the same time implying that the most routine, ordinary tasks, like eating and drinking, should be done to make much of the Lord. Our entire lives should be focused on the purpose of bringing honor and Glory to an awesome God!

Our lives can be lived in one of two ways. Either we honor God with our lives or we dishonor God with our lives. John MacArthur states in his commentary on 1 Corinthians that "God is dishonored when anyone sins, but He is especially dishonored when His own people sin... In the same way God is especially honored and glorified when His people are faithful and obedient." If our freedom in Christ causes us to sin, or anyone else to sin in any way, then God is especially dishonored. If we prevent a brother or sister to bring less glory to God by doing something that is "lawful," then we become disobedient and dishonoring to God. If we prevent an unbeliever from coming to know Christ with our freedom, then we are dishonoring God! In verse 32 Gods word continues, ***"Give no offense to Jews or Greeks or to the church of God."*** This includes all of humanity whether they know Jesus or they do not!

"Give no offense" is echoed in Philippians 1:10-11, ***"so that you may approve what is excellent, and so be pure and blameless for the day of Christ, filled with the fruit of righteousness that comes through Jesus Christ, to the glory and praise of God."*** If our freedom creates offense, impurity, and blame, then God is not glorified or praised! Does the use of our Christian freedom in ALL areas of life glorify God? Do they take away from the glory of God? So, whether we are at work, school, home, church, in the presence of believers or unbelievers, eating, drinking, brushing our teeth, attending the Lion's game, or whatever we are doing, let us do ALL things to the glory of God!

12

THE DEVIL IS IN THE DETAILS

Dr. Randy Johnson | Growth Pastor

Satan is the "Father of Lies". He isn't always blatant in his approach but normally chooses to just twist the truth. Even from the start of the sin in the Garden, we see the Serpent twist what God said to manipulate Eve.

In 1 Corinthians 11, Paul points out two of Satan's target areas: the interdependence of people and the Lord's Supper. Satan tries to cause separation among men and women, husbands and wives, and even Christians with God Himself.

Be imitators of me, as I am of Christ.

What area(s) of your life would you be comfortable with someone imitating you? ____

____

____

2 Now I commend you because you remember me in everything and maintain the traditions even as I delivered them to you. 3 But I want you to understand that the head of every man is Christ, the head of a wife is her husband, and the head of Christ is God. 4 Every man who prays or prophesies with

his head covered dishonors his head, 5 but every wife who prays or prophesies with her head uncovered dishonors her head, since it is the same as if her head were shaven. 6 For if a wife will not cover her head, then she should cut her hair short. But since it is disgraceful for a wife to cut off her hair or shave her head, let her cover her head. 7 For a man ought not to cover his head, since he is the image and glory of God, but woman is the glory of man. 8 For man was not made from woman, but woman from man. 9 Neither was man created for woman, but woman for man. 10 That is why a wife ought to have a symbol of authority on her head, because of the angels. 11 Nevertheless, in the Lord woman is not independent of man nor man of woman; 12 for as woman was made from man, so man is now born of woman. And all things are from God. 13 Judge for yourselves: is it proper for a wife to pray to God with her head uncovered? 14 Does not nature itself teach you that if a man wears long hair it is a disgrace for him, 15 but if a woman has long hair, it is her glory? For her hair is given to her for a covering. 16 If anyone is inclined to be contentious, we have no such practice, nor do the churches of God.

How do we know that the man being the head of his wife doesn't mean he is better or more important than her (verse 3)?

____

____

____

What do verses 8 and 9 refer to? ______________________

____

____

What are the main issues in this passage?

a. A concern for them to give God glory
b. The value and need of both men and women
c. Bald men are beautiful
d. The need for sensitivity to others and culture
e. Women are better than men
f. Men are more important than women

Note: It might be fun to share with each other what different hairstyles you have had through the years.

17 But in the following instructions I do not commend you, because when you come together it is not for the better but for the worse. 18 For, in the first place, when you come together as a church, I hear that there are divisions among you. And I believe it in part, 19 for there must be factions among you in order that those who are genuine among you may be recognized. 20 When you come together, it is not the Lord's supper that you eat. 21 For in eating, each one goes ahead with his own meal. One goes hungry, another gets drunk. 22 What! Do you not have houses to eat and drink in? Or do you despise the church of God and humiliate those who have nothing? What shall I say to you? Shall I commend you in this? No, I will not.

Is it possible to do the right thing in the wrong way (verse 17)?

____

____

____

What was the problem (verses 20-22)? ______________________

____

____

How are people "humiliated" in the church today?

____

____

____

23 For I received from the Lord what I also delivered to you, that the Lord Jesus on the night when he was betrayed took bread, 24 and when he had given thanks, he broke it, and said, "This is my body which is for you. Do this in remembrance of me." 25 In the same way also he took the cup, after supper, saying, "This cup is the new covenant in my blood. Do this, as often as you drink it, in remembrance of me." 26 For as often as you eat this bread and drink the cup, you proclaim the Lord's death until he comes.

Do you have a meal, song, or object that reminds you of a loved one that has passed? ______________________________________

____

____

According to verses 24 and 25, why do we observe the Lord's Supper (Communion, Eucharist)? __________________________

____

____

How is the Lord's Supper helpful in spreading the Gospel (verse 26)? ____

____

____

27 Whoever, therefore, eats the bread or drinks the cup of the Lord in an unworthy manner will be guilty concerning the body and blood of the Lord. 28 Let a person examine

himself, then, and so eat of the bread and drink of the cup. 29 For anyone who eats and drinks without discerning the body eats and drinks judgment on himself. 30 That is why many of you are weak and ill, and some have died. 31 But if we judged ourselves truly, we would not be judged. 32 But when we are judged by the Lord, we are disciplined so that we may not be condemned along with the world.

What are some essential aspects of observing the Lord's Supper (location, elements, number of individuals, attitude…)?

____

____

____

What does it mean to eat in an unworthy manner (verse 27) and what can be the results (verse 30)? ____________________

____

____

33 So then, my brothers, when you come together to eat, wait for one another— 34 if anyone is hungry, let him eat at home—so that when you come together it will not be for judgment. About the other things I will give directions when I come.

How would you explain observing the Lord's Supper to an unbeliever? ____________________________

____

____

"I think the moments we are nearest to heaven are those we spend at the Lord's table." Charles Spurgeon

BE A ROLE MODEL

Jen Combs | Wife of Lead Pastor Josh Combs

1 Corinthians 11:1 says, ***"Be imitators of me, as I am of Christ."*** To understand Paul's beginning statement in chapter 11, we have to go back into chapter 10 to understand what he is saying here. If you just read this and nothing else, I am sure you would just think that Paul was being boastful or prideful in this statement. Remember, context. You cannot just pick a verse out of the Bible and make it say whatever you want. You have to read before and after to understand the point the writer is trying to make. In addition, chapters and verses are not from God. Man put them there to help us organize and find things. This verse is probably better off in chapter 10. Anyway, let's take a look.

At the end of chapter 10, Paul is going over things that were lawful, or ok to do. However, not all things are helpful to you being a light to lost people. Paul cared more about the lost souls than he did about his own liberty. He was willing to give things up that he knew God was ok with so that he could be a light to an unbeliever. He wanted his way of living in no way to hinder someone from seeing Jesus.

Is there something in your life that you need to give up so that unbelievers or young followers of Christ are not distracted? I, in no way, want my life and things I choose to be a hindrance to the Gospel. Matthew 16:23 says, ***"But he (being Jesus) turned and said to Peter, 'Get behind me, Satan! You are a hindrance to me. For you are not setting your mind on the things of God, but the things of man.'"*** Are you caught up in the things of man, rather than God? He was not saying, be just like me because I am sweet and have it all together. Paul was saying, I am willing to give up lots of things in my life for the cause of Christ.

Therefore, I can be all things to all men, not for my glory, but for the glory of Jesus.

What are you willing to give up for the cause of the gospel?

AUTHORITY

Pastor Josh Combs | Lead Pastor

"I want you to understand that the head of every man is Christ, the head of the wife is her husband, and the head of Christ is God" (1 Corinthians 11:3).

Authority is a word and concept that cause most of us bristle. Whether that is our boss, our parents, the police, the president, a building inspector, teacher/professor, or any of the other innumerable authorities in our lives, most of us struggle with authority. Anti-authority is a popular concept and even to some extent respected. However, being anti-authority is unbiblical, and ultimately a sign of the sin of Satan, pride (Isaiah 14:12-15, Ezekiel 28:11).

As a young man, I really struggled with authority. In all honesty, I hated being told what to do by teachers, coaches, and especially the police. When I was 16 years old, I was involved in a car accident where the car I ran into was a patrol car. Yup…that is right. I rear-ended a police officer. Needless to say, he wasn't particularly pleased. From that day on (for reasons I do not have time to explain), I really hated the police. For years, I was disrespectful and rude to them. Through a series of lessons, God drew me to Romans 13, where the Scripture says, ***"…there is no authority except from God, and those that exist have been instituted by God."*** God's Word is very clear about authority. This convicted my heart beyond what I can even convey. My heart towards, not only the police, by all of government, teachers, coaches, pastors, bosses, etc. began to change. In 1 Corinthians, Paul has to teach the importance of and the God-given structure of authority.

First, the Scripture teaches us, that Christ ought to be ***"the head of every man."*** Is Christ your Lord? Your authority? Your Boss? When He speaks, do you listen and obey? In John 14:15, Jesus says, ***"If you love me, you will keep my commandments."*** A sign of genuine salvation is that Jesus is your LORD. That means He calls the shots. That He, as the Bible says, is ***"...the head."***

Secondly, God has given us human authorities. Paul, here in 1 Corinthians speaks to the authority structure of the home. The Bible says, ***"...the head of the wife is her husband...."*** Before you shun the rest of this devotion, realize that this is not a license for husbands to be dictators (Please read Ephesians 5 and 6). Every person is under authority...husbands, wives, and children. The Scripture even speaks extensively to the employee/employer relationship (See 1 Peter 2:13-25).

Lastly, the Scripture says, ***"...the head of Christ is God."*** Philippians 2:6-11, teaches us that Jesus was completely equal with God, but willingly submitted Himself to God the Father. Please catch that...Jesus was EQUAL with God but chose to be submissive to the Father's plan. If Jesus, the creator of the entire universe, can willfully accept a position of submission, then we, learning and strengthened by His example, can do the same.

1 CORINTHIANS 11: DEVOTION 3

CRITICISM CELEBRATED

Pastor Josh Combs | Lead Pastor

"But in the following instructions I do not commend you, because when you come together it is not for the better but for the worse" (1 Corinthians 11:17).

Throughout the book of 1 Corinthians, the Apostle Paul has had to say some pretty serious things to the church at Corinth. He has addressed major divisions within the church, serious immorality, and will in the coming chapters need to address the disaster that ensues when this church gets together. He begins to talk about the mess of their church meetings here in chapter 11. When most Pastors and leaders would be openly and unreservedly encouraging the church to get together, Paul seems to be putting on the brakes. He openly tells these people, things are worse when you get together. That had to hurt…just a little. As we have noted, this is not the first or last tough criticism that Paul must give to these people whom he loves.

There are times when we all must endure criticism. As a Pastor, I have preached some lame sermons and have made countless dumb decisions over the years. Without fail, I have had to endure difficult meetings, where my decisions and/or sermons are put under a very critical microscope. At first, we may be defensive and reluctant to listen to or heed criticism, but we miss a potentially valuable help for our life.

Criticism, even if it is not constructive, can be extremely helpful. I have received critical letters, emails, phone calls, and voicemails. I have been yelled at in private and in the church lobby with lots of people watching. I have had my love for Jesus and for our church questioned by someone I have upset. Criticism is hard but helpful. Here are a few tips on handling criticism.

1. Listen.
James 1 says, ***"...let every person be quick to hear, slow to speak, slow to anger...."*** Before you formulate your response, listen closely. Even crazy people say true things occasionally. Between yelling, tears, or ludicrous accusations, listen, do not miss the potential gold nugget of truth.

2. Confirm the truth before you act or become brokenhearted.
Consider the source. If only one person has this criticism of your life, more than likely it is not true. Deuteronomy 19:15 says, ***"A single witness shall not suffice against a person for any time or for any wrong in connection with any offense that he has committed. Only on the evidence of two witnesses or of three witnesses shall a charge be established."*** So before you make a significant change or become overwhelmed with sorrow, confirm with two or three witnesses that the criticism is true.

3. Thank the person for sharing their concerns.
Always be grateful that someone took the time to share his or her concerns with you. They may have said some untrue things or made wild accusations, but they care enough to share. You may find no support for the criticism, but regardless, be humble enough to begin the conversation assuming you may be wrong.

Every day I pray for God to give me wisdom and discernment (James 1:5). When you confirm that a criticism is valid (discernment), ask the Lord for wisdom on how to change.

RICH AND POOR

Pastor Josh Combs | Lead Pastor

1 Corinthians 11:18-22: ***"For, in the first place, when you come together as a church, I hear that there are divisions among you. And I believe it in part, for there must be factions among you in order that those who are genuine among you may be recognized. When you come together, it is not the Lord's Supper that you eat. For in eating, each one goes ahead with his own meal. One goes hungry, another gets drunk. What! Do you not have houses to eat and drink in? Or do you despise the church of God and humiliate those who have nothing? What shall I say to you? Shall I commend you in this? No, I will not."***

1 Corinthians 33-34: ***"So then, my brothers, when you come together to eat, wait for one another – if anyone is hungry, let him eat at home – so that when you come together it will not be for judgment. About the other things I will give directions when I come."***

The church at Corinth had some serious issues. One of the most difficult and deeply rooted problems they had was class warfare. When the church would get together, the rich would arrive early, while the poor had more difficult schedules, because they had masters (bosses/owners) and many of them were slaves (employees). When the more wealthy members of the church arrived, they would begin to feast. Strangely enough, they would feast on the Lord's Supper (the Agape as it was sometimes called) and when the poor arrived, nothing would be left for them to enjoy. Paul talked very seriously to them about "divisions" and "factions" within the church. Within the Roman Empire, which Corinth was an important part of, divisions amongst people based on class, wealth, and race were common and for the most part accepted. In our American culture, we speak of upper, middle, and lower classes. We celebrate stories of people rising from, for example, lower class into middle or even upper class. However, in Greco-Roman culture, climbing the ladder into another class was not impossible, but extremely rare.

The serious issue in the church was that cultural norms, which were ungodly, had made their way into God's church. Rich despised the poor because that was normal in culture. While the poor, coveted the homes, clothing, and even food of the wealthy. However, the Scripture is crystal clear, ***"...God shows no partiality"*** (Romans 2:11, Acts 10:34). Meaning, God does not play favorites.

History and culture over the last 2,000 years have certainly changed many facets of our life, yet at the same time, so many things remain the same. In James chapter 2, the half-brother of Jesus pleads with the church writing, ***"My brothers, show no partiality as you hold the faith in our Lord Jesus Christ, the Lord of glory."*** As we hold our faith in Jesus, we must let go of our prejudices and let Jesus break down the barriers, between rich and poor, slave and free (Galatians 3:28), educated and uneducated, black and white, and every other "class" that society has put into place. Those barriers and socio-economic classes should have NO place in God's church. We are one, solely because of our Lord Jesus Christ.

From time to time, I like to imagine if Jesus were to walk into one of our Gatherings unexpectedly. He would arrive in modern clothes, but nothing fancy. The Bible says He was a man who did not own a home, walked most places, and didn't on the surface have any attractive qualities (Isaiah 53:2). Would we welcome Him? Would we pass by Him to greet the guy who arrived in nice clothes and a fancy car? In Matthew 25, Jesus says, ***"...as you did it to one of the least of these my brothers, you did it to me."***

REMEMBER AND PROCLAIM

Pastor Josh Combs | Lead Pastor

A precious part of the church and a sacred moment for every believer had been all but obliterated by the church at Corinth. Paul writes, ***"...when you come together, it is NOT the Lord's Supper that you eat."*** The church believed that when they were getting together, they were observing the Lord's Supper, which was instituted by Jesus on the night He was betrayed. However, Paul crushes that assumption, telling that what they were doing was the Lord's Supper in name only. What they were doing was a horrific, ungodly mess that did not come close to resembling what Jesus intended. Therefore, Paul, who was personally instructed by Jesus, takes them back to that sacred night, just hours before the cross of Calvary. Paul writes: ***"For I received from the Lord what I also delivered to you, that the Lord Jesus on the night when he was betrayed took bread, 24 and when he had given thanks, he broke it, and said, 'This is my body which is for you. Do this in remembrance of me.' 25 In the same way also he took the cup, after supper, saying, 'This cup is the new covenant in my blood. Do this, as often as you drink it, in remembrance of me.' 26 For as often as you eat this bread and drink the cup, you proclaim the Lord's death until he comes"*** (1 Corinthians 11:23-26).

Jesus had revealed to His disciples that the Passover was a celebration, not just of freedom of Egyptian bondage, but prophetically to show that God would free us from the significantly greater bondage of sin. He took the cup of wine and the bread. He revealed that the cup with a symbol of the new covenant and that the bread was broken signifying that His body would be broken on the cross. There is little doubt that what Jesus revealed must have left the already confused disciples in deep thought. Paul is writing after the cross and the resurrection, giving the ordinance of the Lord's Supper (communion). There are two key words connected to the Lord's Supper...remember and proclaim.

First, we as believers are always to remember what Jesus did on the cross. We are not to forget the nails that pierced Jesus' hands and feet. We are to remember the crown of thorns, the beatings, the spear, and the great suffering that the Lord endured. As Christians, we must never forget that Christ suffered, paying the penalty for our sin, and satisfying God's righteous wrath.

Secondly, we partake of the Lord's Supper, not only to remember, but also to proclaim. We proclaim that Jesus' death is the only means of peace with God. We proclaim that Jesus died as a willing and innocent sacrifice. We proclaim that Jesus took our place and that through His death we can receive forgiveness of sins. We proclaim that Jesus paid the price in full.

The Lord's Supper is a sacred and solemn time for the church to remember the horrific death of Jesus on the cross. We must never take it lightly or even allow it to become just a tradition. The Lord's Supper must be about remembering and proclaiming.

WARNINGS AND BLESSING

Pastor Josh Combs | Lead Pastor

"Let a person examine himself, then, and so eat of the bread and drink of the cup. For anyone who eats and drinks without discerning the body eats and drinks judgment on himself. That is why many of you are weak and ill, and some have died. But if we judged ourselves truly, we would not be judged. But when we are judged by the Lord, we are disciplined so that we may not be condemned along with the world" (1 Corinthians 11:28-32).

As Paul concludes his instructions to the Corinthians concerning the Lord's Supper, he gives them some extremely serious warnings from the Lord. The Lord's Supper is not to be taken lightly. However, because some had been flippant and careless with communion, they had become ill, and some even died. Before we go any further, we need to realize that these warnings are still in place for Christ's church. When we gather to remember Christ's crucifixion and proclaim the Lord's death, we are to do so with the utmost humility and seriousness. The church is a joyful place, but the irony of the Scripture is expressed in that we are joyful while at the same time somber over the results of sin and the death of our Lord. Before we partake of the Lord's Supper, the Scripture, simply saying, ***"Let a person examine himself..."*** Not only within the context of the Lord's Supper but in all aspects of our life should we be examining ourselves.

I remember as a middle and high school student being very frustrated with my parents' rules. I had a job and for the most part did ok in school. My parents were quite restrictive in certain areas of my life. I will never forget making my case in the laundry room to my Mom one day. The whole premise of my argument was simply, "You should relax on my curfew, because, let's face it, I'm not like the rest of the kids in my high school...I'm way better. You should feel honored to have me has your child." Now, of course, I did not exactly articulate my point that clear or boldly, but nonetheless, that was my thesis. Against, the principle of Scripture, I was examining myself in the light of others. The Bible often warns against comparative righteous...meaning that we can always find someone who is "worse" than us to justify how bad we are and then conclude we are kind of awesome.

The whole idea of the Lord's Supper is an exercise in going to the cross and remembering and proclaiming. Remembering not just how Christ died, but that our sin against God put him there. That should be a very humbling, not prideful, reality. When we "examine" ourselves, we ought not to look around and compare to others, but compare our life to Christ, through the Scripture. It is much easier and less painful to compare to others around us who we deem less godly than we are. However, within the light of the Scripture, we see ourselves, as we really are, broken, sinful, and helpless. When this examination is done at the foot of the cross, we are quickly encouraged and lifted up, because Jesus took all of that and much more on Himself at the Cross.

13

DEM DRY BONES

Dr. Randy Johnson | Growth Pastor

Do you remember the song, "Dem Dry Bones"?

Earlier, the Corinthians were arguing over which leader (Paul, Apollos, Cephas) was best. Now, we will realize they also argued over who had which spiritual gifts, responsibilities, and, therefore, was more important. Paul emphasizes the importance of every gift and every believer.

Now concerning spiritual gifts, brothers, I do not want you to be uninformed. 2 You know that when you were pagans you were led astray to mute idols, however you were led. 3 Therefore I want you to understand that no one speaking in the Spirit of God ever says "Jesus is accursed!" and no one can say "Jesus is Lord" except in the Holy Spirit.

What do you already know about spiritual gifts?

___

___

___

"When you find your spiritual gift, God will give you an opportunity to use it." John C. Maxwell

4 Now there are varieties of gifts, but the same Spirit; 5 and there are varieties of service, but the same Lord; 6 and there are varieties of activities, but it is the same God who empowers them all in everyone. 7 To each is given the manifestation of the Spirit for the common good. 8 For to one is given through the Spirit the utterance of wisdom, and to another the utterance of knowledge according to the same Spirit, 9 to another faith by the same Spirit, to another gifts of healing by the one Spirit, 10 to another the working of miracles, to another prophecy, to another the ability to distinguish between spirits, to another various kinds of tongues, to another the interpretation of tongues. 11 All these are empowered by one and the same Spirit, who apportions to each one individually as he wills.

"Having gifts that differ according to the grace given to us, let us use them: if prophecy, in proportion to our faith; 7 if service, in our serving; the one who teaches, in his teaching; 8 the one who exhorts, in his exhortation; the one who contributes, in generosity; the one who leads, with zeal; the one who does acts of mercy, with cheerfulness" (Romans 12:6-8).

"And he gave the apostles, the prophets, the evangelists, the shepherds and teachers" (Ephesians 4:11).

"As each has received a gift, use it to serve one another, as good stewards of God's varied grace: 11 whoever speaks, as one who speaks oracles of God; whoever serves, as one who serves by the strength that God supplies—in order that in everything God may be glorified through Jesus Christ. To him belong glory and dominion forever and ever. Amen" (1 Peter 4:10-11).

These are the key verses (along with 1 Corinthians 12:28-30) that list spiritual gifts. List the different spiritual gifts.

____

____

____

Which spiritual gift(s) do you have? ____________________

____

____

Can you see the Trinity at work in these verses (4-6)?

____

____

____

12 For just as the body is one and has many members, and all the members of the body, though many, are one body, so it is with Christ. 13 For in one Spirit we were all baptized into one body—Jews or Greeks, slaves or free—and all were made to drink of one Spirit.
14 For the body does not consist of one member but of many. 15 If the foot should say, "Because I am not a hand, I do not belong to the body," that would not make it any less a part of the body. 16 And if the ear should say, "Because I am not an eye, I do not belong to the body," that would not make it any less a part of the body. 17 If the whole body were an eye, where would be the sense of hearing? If the whole body were an ear, where would be the sense of smell? 18 But as it is, God arranged the members in the body, each one of them, as he chose. 19 If all were a single member, where would the body be? 20 As it is, there are many parts, yet one body.

Paul uses the body as an illustration. What illustration of needing each other do you see in your life (sports, music, technology, recipe...)? ______________________________

____

____

"Some people have a warped idea of living the Christian life. Seeing talented, successful Christians, they attempt to imitate them. For them, the grass on the other side of the fence is always greener. But when they discover that their own gifts are different or their contributions are more modest (or even invisible), they collapse in discouragement and overlook genuine opportunities that are open to them. They have forgotten that they are here to serve Christ, not themselves." Billy Graham

21 The eye cannot say to the hand, "I have no need of you," nor again the head to the feet, "I have no need of you." 22 On the contrary, the parts of the body that seem to be weaker are indispensable, 23 and on those parts of the body that we think less honorable we bestow the greater honor, and our unpresentable parts are treated with greater modesty, 24 which our more presentable parts do not require. But God has so composed the body, giving greater honor to the part that lacked it, 25 that there may be no division in the body, but that the members may have the same care for one another. 26 If one member suffers, all suffer together; if one member is honored, all rejoice together.

Which spiritual gifts are possibly viewed as unpresentable and which would be considered presentable? ______________________________

____

____

How can we show more respect to those whose spiritual gift may be viewed as unpresentable? ______________________________

____

____

"As God's children, we are not to be observers; we're to participate actively in the Lord's work. Spectators sit and watch, but we are called to use our spiritual gifts and serve continually."
Charles Stanley

27 Now you are the body of Christ and individually members of it. 28 And God has appointed in the church first apostles, second prophets, third teachers, then miracles, then gifts of healing, helping, administrating, and various kinds of tongues. 29 Are all apostles? Are all prophets? Are all teachers? Do all work miracles? 30 Do all possess gifts of healing? Do all speak with tongues? Do all interpret? 31 But earnestly desire the higher gifts.
And I will show you a still more excellent way.

Earlier you listed the different spiritual gifts. Do you think the list is exclusive? If not, what other "gifts" have you seen in the church? ____

____

____

"[The remaining] works of the Holy Spirit which are at this time vouchsafed to the Church of God are, in every way, as valuable as those earlier miraculous gifts which have departed from us. The work of the Holy Spirit, by which men are quickened from their death in sin, is not inferior to the power which made men speak with tongues! The work of the Holy Spirit, when He comforts men and makes them glad in Christ, is by no means second to the opening of the eyes of the blind!" Charles Spurgeon

FAMILY TALK

Noble Baird | Director of Guest Services

As followers of Christ, we are one big family. Although we are not all related through blood, we are related through the blood of Christ. It is through that family mindset that Paul is writing to the church in Corinth. Just as our biological families have issues and struggles; the same is true of our family in Christ.

In 1 Corinthians 12, Paul brings up the topic of spiritual gifts. Sadly, this topic has become misunderstood and misconstrued by many. Because of this, Paul wants to make sure that his "family" is not uninformed. In 12:1-3, Paul writes about the importance of not being led astray. He explains the power of the Holy Spirit and how no one can declare Jesus is Lord, except those who have the Holy Spirit living in him or her.

In today's world, it is easy to claim ignorance and find some excuse for not having time. As followers of Christ, we are called to spread His Word. Even though families can fight and bicker, at the end of the day, family is family. Although we do not see eye to eye on certain topics, there is nothing I would not do for my cousin Trever. Likewise, the same must be true of our brothers and sisters in Christ. It is out of this love for his family in Christ, which includes us, which Paul wants to make sure we are not ignorant and uninformed of these truths about the Holy Spirit.

As we take this week to dig a little deeper into this chapter of Corinthians, I challenge you not to be ignorant. Sure, you can skim over these devotionals and study guides because there is nothing special about them or the people who wrote them. However, if you choose to skim over God's Word and what He has placed in this amazing book called the Bible, then you are missing it all. As your brother in Christ, family, I do not want you to be ignorantly uninformed about His Spirit and Word.

GIFTS FOR COMMON GOOD

Noble Baird | Director of Guest Services

The common good - a phrase that is often thrown around by many today. We constantly hear it from our politicians, new reporters, and motivational speakers. However, once all the hyperbole dies down, the actions always speak louder than the words. Sadly, in this case, the true common good is often lost in translation and focus is reverted to self.

In 1 Corinthians 12:4-7, Paul writes about this common good. He explains how, as followers of Christ, we are all given special gifts and talents. For some that may be preaching or teaching, others it is singing or maintenance work. Whatever your gift is, it has been given to you on purpose. The abilities, talents, and skills you have are not a mistake. Paul writes clearly in verse 7, ***"To each is given the manifestation of the Spirit for the common good."***

Now, here comes the hard part, your decision. For many of you reading this, you already know the gifts and talents you have. Others are still trying to figure it out and that is okay, keep searching! However, no matter if you already know or are still searching, you must decide whom you will use those gifts and talents for. Are you going to use those gifts for your personal gain? Will you use them to glorify the One who gave you the gifts, so that you can be used to benefit all? Remember, your actions speak louder than your words.

TEAMWORK

Noble Baird | Director of Guest Services

"There is no 'I' in 'team." I have always loved this quote. Whether you are in a multimillion-dollar corporation, on a football team, or a teacher in your school district, teamwork is an essential part of life. A couple of weeks ago, I had the opportunity to help put up banners over at the Eastern Michigan football stadium. I honestly had no idea what I was getting into, but I am always up for a new adventure! For nine hours straight, a team of six of us went up and down the bleachers ratcheting and securing massive banners across the stadium. While we were securing the banners, we had to have two people at the top of the banner and one at the bottom. Once the top of the banner was secured, the person at the bottom would secure the middle. After this, we would slowly work our way from the middle to the sides of the bottom. While doing this, one person would watch for the creases so the people at the top and bottom could ratchet the banner to work out the creases.

One of my favorite verses in the Bible is 1 Corinthians 12:12, ***"For just as the body is one and has many members, and all the members of the body, though many, are one body, so it is with Christ."*** I love this passage because of the idea of a team that Paul portrays. None of us are in this life alone. Yes, at times we may feel beat down and subdued by the hardships of this world, but no matter how hard it gets we are never alone. When Paul writes about this "one body," he is referring to the family that we are in Christ. That family I was telling you about the other day, this is it! We are one body, one family, and one team, in Christ!

I will be honest with you, putting those banners across the stadium was some of the hardest work I have had to do. Even though it was rough and I hated it at times, I could not even imagine what it would have been like to do it alone...impossible! I was part of a team; we were a group of people who had never worked together before. However, we were each given a task, and we worked together as a team to complete that task. We came together as one, and the outcome was a success. As followers of Christ, we cannot do this life alone. Just as a football team, corporation, or school cannot succeed with just one person, the same is true of the Church. So, I challenge you to get involved. Yes, I understand everyone has a busy schedule, but we can all find time to give back in some way, shape, or form. Whether it is coming in on a Friday night and preparing the auditorium for our gathering on the weekend. Maybe it is going downtown and helping Miss Pat sort some clothing for just an hour, every little bit helps! We are one body in Christ, and since there is no 'I' in team, we need you!

BAND TOGETHER

Noble Baird | Director of Guest Services

One of my biggest passions is music. Ever since I was a child, my father has always been playing some type of Rock n Roll! Whether it was Led Zeppelin, Def Leppard, ZZ Top, KISS, The Rolling Stones, or my all-time favorite, The Beatles, music has always been a part of my life. One band in particular that has fascinated me by not only their musical ability but by their longevity is The Rolling Stones. For over 50 years, the Stones have been performing, recording, and touring all over the world together. Yes, they have had their share of struggles and hardships; however, they have stuck together and have continued to push through. Their lead guitarist Keith Richards even said, "The only way to quit will be in a coffin." That is a pretty strong statement, but time has shown it to be true. No matter what has happened, they have taken care of each other and have settled whatever issues arise; they have not quit on each other.

As Paul writes about this one body that we are in Christ, he writes about the importance of being unified. In 1 Corinthians 12:21-25, Paul writes about how each of us is an integral part of the body. He says in 12:24-25, ***"But God has so composed the body, giving greater honor to the part that lacked it, that there may be no division in the body, but that the members may have the same care for one another."*** In other words, it does not matter if you are on the stage Sunday morning, standing at the main entrance to the auditorium, or holding a baby back in the nursery, you are an integral part of the body...an integral part that we need!

Just as the Stones have not let any issues or struggles divide them over the past 50 years, the same is true of us as the Body of Christ. Paul says it right at the end of verse 25; we must care for one another. Part of caring for one another is not letting any of those hardships or issues divide us. We have been talking about this idea of being a team and a family for the past couple days. As we continue to move forward: serving together, worshiping together, digging into God's Word together, and simply living this life together, we must care for one another. We must remember that none of us are more important or valuable than our brothers and sisters in Christ. So, as you go throughout this week, I challenge you to take time and care for one another. Send someone an encouraging text, write a letter, buy him or her a gift card to Starbucks, whatever you can think of! Just send that someone a little something to let him or her know that you care and they are important!

1 CORINTHIANS 12: DEVOTION 5

PUMPKIN BREAD

Noble Baird | Director of Guest Services

I love dessert. As a kid, I would always make sure I finished my meal so that I could have dessert afterward. Now, one of my most favorite desserts ever is pumpkin bread. I love pretty much anything pumpkin: pie, cupcakes, ice cream, but pumpkin bread is one of my top five favorite desserts. With that said, at the end of this devotional, I have included a special recipe. I was given the privilege to share this recipe with all of you from Ang Wyer so that you could make some amazing pumpkin bread. However, just like dinner, you have to finish the devotional first to get to it!

All throughout 1 Corinthians 12, Paul is writing about this concept of unity in Christ. He is writing about whom we are in Christ, finding our gifts and talents, and using those gifts to work together with our fellow brothers and sisters to glorify God. In 1 Corinthians 12:26 Paul writes, ***"If one member suffers, all suffer together; if one member is honored, all rejoice together."*** It is this concept of oneness that we must remember as we press forward following God's will for our lives. When we have a baptism at church, it is an exciting time. Everyone is clapping, shouting, and praising God for the work He is doing in that brother or sister of ours. In the same way, when one of our brothers or sisters is in the hospital or struggling through hard times, we come beside them and share in their grief or pain.

As I mentioned before, I love pumpkin bread, but if one ingredient is wrong or missing, the whole thing tastes bad. In the same way, as followers of Christ, we need each other. We are one body for a reason; everyone matters. If we are missing one person or someone is not using the gift he or she has been given, then that unity is hindered. Yes, we are to rejoice when a brother or sister is honored, or we receive a new brother or sister in Christ. However, if one is hurting and suffering, we need to come beside them and be with them. We need to visit them in the hospital, stop by their house with a meal or a dessert, or simply give them a call and pray with them. No matter if it is in rejoicing or suffering, we must never forget to do it together, as one in Christ.

Pumpkin Bread:
3 cups pumpkin purée
1.5 cups vegetable or canola oil
4 cups sugar
6 eggs
4.75 cups flour
1.5 tsp of baking powder
1.5 tsp baking soda
1.5 tsp of salt
4.5 tsp pumpkin pie spice (if not available divide between nutmeg, clove, and cinnamon)

Mix pumpkin, eggs, sugar, and oil until blended. Mix in all dry ingredients.

Top, when cooked, with powdered sugar glaze (if too thick gradually add small amounts of milk until desired consistency):

2 cups powder sugar
1/2 tsp vanilla
3 tsp of milk

Bake at 350 for 40-60 minutes depending on pan size. Test with toothpick.

Yields 3 large loaf pans or 10 little loaf pans.

ANSWER THE CALL

Noble Baird | Director of Guest Services

Over this past week, we have taken a deeper look into 1 Corinthians 12. If there was one passage that sums up this whole idea of unity in Christ, it is found in 1 Corinthians 12:27. Paul writes, ***"Now you are the body of Christ and individually members of it."*** As I was preparing and writing the devotionals for this week, I began to get a little worried. While working my way through this chapter, I realized how much Paul reiterates this concept of unity and being one body in Christ. That said, I did not want to sound redundant. However, I realized that if Paul found it necessary to reiterate this concept so much throughout this entire chapter, it must be pretty important!

Calling. By definition calling is, "a strong desire to spend your life doing a certain kind of work; the work that a person does or should be doing." For a majority of my life, this word meant nothing. I often heard it thrown around by the pastors I would listen to or my teachers at Oakland Christian School. Yet honestly, some of my biggest concerns were what my friends and I were doing later on or when was church over. It was not until a trip down to Atlanta, Georgia to walk the streets praying with some homeless people I had never met before that this whole "calling" thing began to make sense.

Atlanta was the last place on earth I ever expected to have my life changed in, but it happened. I was with a group of kids from my youth group who I barely knew, but they accepted me. I thought it would simply be a warm getaway from Michigan, but it ended up turning my world upside down. You see, between the love I was shown by random people on the streets of Atlanta who only owned the clothing on their backs and the group of my peers who I barely knew, that word was beginning to become illuminated in my life. For the first time, I was starting to see a purpose for my life. This purpose was not found looking through my eyes but through the eyes of Christ.

I was challenged during that week. To say my world was rocked is a pretty accurate statement. Although at that moment I had no idea God would eventually take me to Chicago to attend a Bible college, then lead me back to the little town I had lived in for over 15 years now to serve in full-time ministry; I did find my calling. I understood that there was a desire in me, and I needed simply to trust Him. It was from that short week in Atlanta that I finally understood what it meant not only to be a part of this amazing body of Christ but what it meant to find my calling.

So, after all this week, all these devotionals, and all this time we spent looking over 1 Corinthians 12, I want to leave you with one last challenge. Simply, have you found your calling? Have you found the desire of your heart? Can you honestly wake up every day and say that you are about to go work or serve where your heart burns? It is okay if the answer is no, which is why I am asking...it is a tough question! However, never forget that we are all in this together. We are here to love, laugh, serve, support, encourage, struggle beside, and face the hardships of this life together. One body, one family united in Christ.

14

"ALL WE NEED IS..."

Dr. Randy Johnson | Growth Pastor

This is known as the LOVE chapter. Some of these verses are implemented into numerous wedding ceremonies.

1 Corinthians 12 spoke about spiritual gifts; chapter 14 specifically covers prophecy and speaking in tongues.

Why do you think this chapter is sandwiched between the other two? ____

____

____

"Spiritual gifts have to do with God-given abilities. Spiritual ministries, like love, are everyone's responsibility." Chuck Swindoll

If I speak in the tongues of men and of angels, but have not love, I am a noisy gong or a clanging cymbal. 2 And if I have prophetic powers, and understand all mysteries and all knowledge, and if I have all faith, so as to remove mountains, but have not love, I am nothing. 3 If I give away all I have, and if I deliver up my body to be burned, but have not love, I gain nothing.

Greek has different words that are translated "love" in English. This passage uses the word "agape" (unconditional love as God has for us). Other Greek words translated love are: "storge" (love between parent and child), "philia" (brotherly love for friends and relatives), and "eros" (the intimate love between husband and wife). Do you think these kinds of love can overlap?

____

____

____

Give an example how an apparently good work actually isn't because it was not done in love? ____________________

____

____

"You can always give without loving, but you can never love without giving." Amy Carmichael

4 Love is patient and kind; love does not envy or boast; it is not arrogant 5 or rude. It does not insist on its own way; it is not irritable or resentful; 6 it does not rejoice at wrongdoing, but rejoices with the truth. 7 Love bears all things, believes all things, hopes all things, endures all things.

Which description is most meaningful to you?

____

____

____

What other characteristic of love would you add?

____

____

____

Which description is hardest to practice consistently?

____

____

____

8 Love never ends. As for prophecies, they will pass away; as for tongues, they will cease; as for knowledge, it will pass away. 9 For we know in part and we prophesy in part, 10 but when the perfect comes, the partial will pass away. 11 When I was a child, I spoke like a child, I thought like a child, I reasoned like a child. When I became a man, I gave up childish ways. 12 For now we see in a mirror dimly, but then face to face. Now I know in part; then I shall know fully, even as I have been fully known.

What three gifts of the Spirit will pass away or cease (verse 8)?

____

____

____

The phrase when the perfect comes, the partial will pass away has brought about many discussions. All agree that the gifts of prophecy, tongues, and knowledge will cease, but when? Some believe the perfect refers to the return of Jesus Christ. Others believe it is the establishment of the church. Finally, I believe it is the completed New Testament at the end of the apostolic age around 100 AD. (In Greek, the article before a word has a gender associated to it. The article before perfect is in the neuter tense - Jesus would be masculine and the church would be feminine). Some gifts were "sign gifts" validating the apostles. However, the sign gifts can still happen where the scripture is absent.

How is having the complete Word of God more valuable than having some people with the gifts of prophecy, tongues, and knowledge? ____

____

____

13 So now faith, hope, and love abide, these three; but the greatest of these is love.

How is love greater than faith and hope? Is there a difference in the self-focus or outward focus? ___________________________

____

____

"If we have got the true love of God shed abroad in our hearts, we will show it in our lives. We will not have to go up and down the earth proclaiming it. We will show it in everything we say or do." Dwight L. Moody

"The best use of life is love. The best expression of love is time. The best time to love is now." Rick Warren

WHAT IS LOVE?

Pastor Ty Woznek | Pastor's Academy Lead Instructor

Paul says, ***"If I speak in the tongues of men and of angels, but have not love, I am a noisy gong or a clanging cymbal. And if I have prophetic powers, and understand all mysteries and all knowledge, and if I have all faith, so as to remove mountains, but have not love, I am nothing. If I give away all I have, and if I deliver up my body to be burned, but have not love, I gain nothing."***

Love is not what we often think
If we do not love, then what we do matters not. There are many successful people who are nobodies because they lack what Paul calls "the most excellent way." Put simply, if we are a super hero, but lack love, then we are nothing.

Defining love
Many have various definition of love. Love sacrifices, but love is not sacrifice. Love does epic things, but epic things do not make for love. What makes love profound is its focus. Not merely an action put on the recipient.

Pride
Pride is the opposite of love. Pride sacrifices, but pride is not sacrifice. Pride does epic things, but epic things do not make for love. What makes pride dangerous is our self-focus. We could care less about others.

Pride versus love
A well to do couple was celebrating their anniversary. The wife was a darling, but the husband was often despised. How could such a gracious woman live with such an arrogant man? Eventually

some of the wives mustered the courage to ask the wife, "How could you stay married to that man?" "Simple," she replied, "We both love the same person."

What is love?
This week we will focus on what Paul says love IS. He gives us a beautiful description including both what love is not and what it is. The descriptions of what love is not, centers on pride. The descriptions of what love is centers on selflessness. What we will see is that love is something we all want but do not like to give. Love is hard work, but anything that is of excellence is.

BE PATIENT

Pastor Ty Woznek | Pastor's Academy Lead Instructor

Paul says, ***"Love is patient."***

Rabbit sings
"I just wanna have patience, cause patience is a wonderful thing. Hurry up, gotta have it! I want it more than anything! This has taken long enough, give me some of that patience stuff!"

The Challenge
My younger sister would play a tape over and over again. She loved to play that song, or, she was just annoying me. Likely both. The "be patient" thing does not work. Seriously. I am 37 years old at the time of writing this, and that song is still stuck in my head. Every time I hear the word patience, I cannot help but sing it. Then there are those who pray for patience. That is proof of a lack of wisdom on our part. God will place things in our life that will produce patience.

You want it, but not give it
You and I get frustrated with people when they are not patient with us. You and I get frustrated when we have to be patient with other people. (Ok, I'm sure someone reading this may not struggle with this. The Bible does say angels show up once in awhile.) We live in a hurried society focused on convenience. Something has to be broken down to practice patience. Then we blame.

God, others, you
The key to patience is resting in God. If we truly believe God has a plan for our lives (HE DOES! Psalm 139, Ephesians 2:10), then circumstances in our life are under his control. He understands and knows what is going on. Frustrating times in life then become

learning opportunities. If God is our focus, then seeking how to bless people comes in line as well. After all, if God can forgive us, why not show the same grace towards others? We cannot be patient if we are the center of our universe.

When you want to a) Scream b) Swear c) Throw something d) ALL THE ABOVE, ask yourself this question: What is God teaching me in this circumstance? We cannot control life; we can only control how we respond to life's challenges. Patience is a choice we make to see what God is teaching us. Lack of patience is a sign that we are placing ourselves at the center, and that is dangerous.

BE KIND

Pastor Ty Woznek | Pastor's Academy Lead Instructor

Paul says, ***"Love is kind."***

Oompa Loompas sing
Oompa loompa doompety da
If you're not spoiled then you will go far
You will live in happiness too
Like the Oompa Loompa Doompety do

The Challenge
Election years mean kindness goes out the window. We get very frustrated by the lack of civility. Such is a growing problem, but also one that existed for quite some time. When driving, shopping, eating at restaurants, we are not always known for our kindness. At the grocery store I worked at in college, the saying went, "Sunday's are great, and then church lets out." Then there is the joke, "What is the difference between a Baptist and a canoe? A canoe at least tips once in a while." Having grown up in a Baptist church, ouch.

You want it, but not give it
It is easy to receive kindness. We all want to receive it. We love movies about it, like "Pay It Forward." Then why do we not want to give it? The reality is it takes work and choosing to be disrupted. Lack of kindness is the path of least resistance, but it is also the path of most blessings. We excuse kindness in so many ways, but it can leave such a massive impact.

God, Others, You
Paul tells us in Ephesians to be kind to one another, tenderhearted. Why? Because God in Christ Jesus forgave us! Our response to

the Gospel is to be kind to one another. Our love for one another is the foundation to reach those who do not know Christ. Rick Warren says it well, “It’s hard to reach your enemies to Christ, it’s much easier to win your friends.” The solution is kindness. Put others before yourself. Be gracious.

When you want to get even…
Ask yourself regularly this question: How can I bless others in this situation? We cannot control people, only how we respond to them. Kindness is a choice we make in light of what God did for us. Lack of kindness is a sign we have forgotten the HUGE kindness shown to us in Christ Jesus. Be like Jesus and show kindness.

1 CORINTHIANS 13: DEVOTION 4

BEAR ALL THINGS

Pastor Ty Woznek | Pastor's Academy Lead Instructor

Paul says, ***"Love bears all things."***

Savage Garden sings, "Let me be the one you call, if you jump I'll break your fall, Lift you up and fly away with you into the night. If you need to fall apart, I can mend a broken heart. If you need to crash then crash and burn, you're not alone."

The Challenge
People can drain us. They take time. Turning lives around is no small feat and takes incredible amounts of work, time, and sacrifice. When things fall apart in a person's life, we argue and scream internally at what is going on. To quote a book title, Love is the Killer App; it is the difference between making it or not. It is called bearing all things.

You want it, but not give it
Bearing all things takes sacrifice. Period. It means being inconvenienced. It means experiencing pain with someone. It means listening. It means shutting off our phone and being present. In a technology-filled world, we are more disconnected and alone. We need people. God knew this. He designed us for relationships. When life is turned upside-down is when people are needed most.

God, Others, You
Paul says that perfect love is that a man lay down his life for a friend. God did that on our behalf. When Jesus gave us communion as a reminder, the bread is significant. Jesus gave Himself for us. Jesus served. The Holy Spirit, whom we received when we asked Jesus to save us, even prays on our behalf when we do not

know how to pray. God sticks with us. God never leaves us. Once saved, we are adopted into a new family, the church. This family comprised of broken and redeemed people like you and like me.

When you want to run…
Ask yourself this question regularly, "How can I be there for people in this situation?" We cannot control other people's circumstances, only how we respond to them. Bearing all things is a choice we make in light of God, who stands by us. Not bearing all things is a sign we have forgotten people matter most to Jesus. Be like Jesus and bear with people through their trials.

BE POSITIVE

Pastor Ty Woznek | Pastor's Academy Lead Instructor

Paul says, ***"Love believes all things, hopes all things."***

R. Kelly sings, "I used to think that I could not go on, And life was nothing but an awful song.
But now I know the meaning of true love, I'm leaning on the everlasting arms."

The Challenge
Love takes courage and a positive attitude. Too often, we cringe at the idea of being positive. Being positive is not a garden of roses. Being positive is seeing a sticky situation and working toward a solution to make it better. A loving person assumes the best unless proved otherwise. It is the relationship version of innocent until proven guilty. It means to focus on what we can learn from a person rather than see faults all the time.

You want it, but not give it
A church I worked at held to no drinking. I was shocked to see a lady from church walking out of a liquor store. This was not good, I thought. The family invited me over for dinner to thank me for my ministry. She made the most amazing bourbon chicken ever. I saw the bottle. Had I gone in and addressed what I saw, "How could you be drinking!?" I would have destroyed what was a pleasant evening. We want people to assume the best in us, and we should do the same. Things are not always what they seem.

God, Others, You
I think if we were honest, most Christians would say no if they were asked deep down do they believe God loves them. We know how broken we are, think, or can be. God does something amazing

to us. He does not condemn us. He saves us. See, God can believe and hope all things in us because of the work He did for us. There is no sin too great God cannot forgive. However, we are not perfect. Nor is our perspective always accurate. Being positive is not ignoring sin in others; it is assuming best first and when shown otherwise seeing what God can do to redeem the situation.

When you think you're right, and they're wrong…
Ask yourself this question regularly, "How sure am I that I am right, and how important is it?" Our perception is not always right, so we must be careful how we respond to what we see. Being positive is a choice we make in light of our limited perspective and also God's amazing grace. Not being positive is a sign we have a critical or embittered spirit. We should try to be like Jesus and see the best in people and what they can become. We should not ignore sin, but instead see what grace can do in a sinner's life.

ENDURE

Pastor Ty Woznek | Pastor's Academy Lead Instructor

Paul says, ***"Love endures all things."***

We sing, "His oath, his covenant, his blood
supports me in the whelming flood.
When all around my soul gives way,
he then is all my hope and stay."

The Challenge
Life is hard and not fair. Responsibility, a sign of adulthood, is not always fun. Putting up with people's faults is annoying. This is what the writer of Ecclesiastes had in mind when he wrote that poetic book. Life on Earth without God in the picture makes no sense. However, key to love is endurance.

Don't give up
The bottom line is love does not give up. It is not a hormonal, twitterpated feeling. Love is a deep-rooted commitment to something beyond you that does not, nor will not quit. Core to love is commitment and promise. Those federal grounds are where love flourishes. Love puts up with a lot because it knows what God can do if we do not give up.

God, Others, You
The Bible says in Second Timothy that if we are faithless, God remains faithful because He cannot deny Himself. We are secure in our relationship with God. He loves us that much. This is why love is the greater way. While there may be hard things we have to do because love requires it, biblical love does not give up. The core issue is the choice you make.

Love is…
Patient. Ask yourself this question regularly, “What is God teaching me in this circumstance?”
Kind. Ask yourself this question regularly, “How can I bless others in this situation?”
Bears all things. Ask yourself this question regularly, “How can I be there for people in this situation?”
Positive. Ask yourself this question regularly, “How sure am I that I am right and how important is it?”
Endures. Don’t give up! We do not always understand why things happen, but we do understand that God is in control.

Based on this truth, love hangs on. In the end, there is only love as faith and hope are fulfilled when Jesus returns. When Jesus returns, we will love perfectly. If we struggle with endurance, then it is a good sign we need people in our life to help carry us, for we should not love alone. Even Moses had Joshua and Caleb to hold his hands up as he endured in prayer.

WEEK 14

15

TONGUE TIED

Dr. Randy Johnson | Growth Pastor

Chapter 13 reminded us of the foundation of love. This chapter discusses prophecy, speaking in tongues, and then emphasizes orderly conduct in public worship.

"The laity ought to understand the faith, and since the doctrines of our faith are in the Scriptures, believers should have the Scriptures in a language familiar to the people, and to this end the Holy Ghost endued them with knowledge of all tongues." John Wycliffe

Pursue love, and earnestly desire the spiritual gifts, especially that you may prophesy. 2 For one who speaks in a tongue speaks not to men but to God; for no one understands him, but he utters mysteries in the Spirit. 3 On the other hand, the one who prophesies speaks to people for their upbuilding and encouragement and consolation. 4 The one who speaks in a tongue builds up himself, but the one who prophesies builds up the church. 5 Now I want you all to speak in tongues, but even more to prophesy. The one who prophesies is greater than the one who speaks in tongues, unless someone interprets, so that the church may be built up.

How are the first two words, pursue love, to be applied in the church? ___

___

___

What is the negative aspect of tongues (verse 4)?

___

___

___

What is the goal of spiritual gifts (verse 5)? ___

___

___

6 Now, brothers, if I come to you speaking in tongues, how will I benefit you unless I bring you some revelation or knowledge or prophecy or teaching? 7 If even lifeless instruments, such as the flute or the harp, do not give distinct notes, how will anyone know what is played? 8 And if the bugle gives an indistinct sound, who will get ready for battle? 9 So with yourselves, if with your tongue you utter speech that is not intelligible, how will anyone know what is said? For you will be speaking into the air. 10 There are doubtless many different languages in the world, and none is without meaning, 11 but if I do not know the meaning of the language, I will be a foreigner to the speaker and the speaker a foreigner to me. 12 So with yourselves, since you are eager for manifestations of the Spirit, strive to excel in building up the church.

The Corinthians struggled with pride. How could some of the gifts get us off a correct focus? ___

___

____

____

"Going to church doesn't make you a Christian any more than going to a garage makes you an automobile." Billy Sunday

13 Therefore, one who speaks in a tongue should pray that he may interpret. 14 For if I pray in a tongue, my spirit prays but my mind is unfruitful. 15 What am I to do? I will pray with my spirit, but I will pray with my mind also; I will sing praise with my spirit, but I will sing with my mind also. 16 Otherwise, if you give thanks with your spirit, how can anyone in the position of an outsider say "Amen" to your thanksgiving when he does not know what you are saying? 17 For you may be giving thanks well enough, but the other person is not being built up. 18 I thank God that I speak in tongues more than all of you. 19 Nevertheless, in church I would rather speak five words with my mind in order to instruct others, than ten thousand words in a tongue.

How is the mind of the worshipper to be involved in worship?

____

____

____

Explain verse 19. ____________________________________

____

____

20 Brothers, do not be children in your thinking. Be infants in evil, but in your thinking be mature. 21 In the Law it is written, "By people of strange tongues and by the lips of foreigners will I speak to this people, and even then they

will not listen to me, says the Lord." 22 Thus tongues are a sign not for believers but for unbelievers, while prophecy is a sign not for unbelievers but for believers. 23 If, therefore, the whole church comes together and all speak in tongues, and outsiders or unbelievers enter, will they not say that you are out of your minds? 24 But if all prophesy, and an unbeliever or outsider enters, he is convicted by all, he is called to account by all, 25 the secrets of his heart are disclosed, and so, falling on his face, he will worship God and declare that God is really among you.

Explain verse 20 in the church setting and in general life.

___

___

___

26 What then, brothers? When you come together, each one has a hymn, a lesson, a revelation, a tongue, or an interpretation. Let all things be done for building up. 27 If any speak in a tongue, let there be only two or at most three, and each in turn, and let someone interpret. 28 But if there is no one to interpret, let each of them keep silent in church and speak to himself and to God. 29 Let two or three prophets speak, and let the others weigh what is said. 30 If a revelation is made to another sitting there, let the first be silent. 31 For you can all prophesy one by one, so that all may learn and all be encouraged, 32 and the spirits of prophets are subject to prophets. 33 For God is not a God of confusion but of peace.

Paul says God is not a God of confusion (verse 33); are there aspects where your church gatherings display confusion or lack peace? ___

____

____

As in all the churches of the saints, 34 the women should keep silent in the churches. For they are not permitted to speak, but should be in submission, as the Law also says. 35 If there is anything they desire to learn, let them ask their husbands at home. For it is shameful for a woman to speak in church.

Why would Paul say women should keep silent (verse 34)?

____

____

____

36 Or was it from you that the word of God came? Or are you the only ones it has reached? 37 If anyone thinks that he is a prophet, or spiritual, he should acknowledge that the things I am writing to you are a command of the Lord. 38 If anyone does not recognize this, he is not recognized. 39 So, my brothers, earnestly desire to prophesy, and do not forbid speaking in tongues. 40 But all things should be done decently and in order.

What are the basic guidelines regarding the use of spiritual gifts in gatherings?

Verses 5, 12, and 26: ______________________________

____

Verse 20: ______________________________________

____

Verses 33 and 40: ____

____

"Wherever we see the Word of God purely preached and heard, there a church of God exists, even if it swarms with many faults." John Calvin

1 CORINTHIANS 14: DEVOTION 1

PROPHESY IN LOVE

Donna Fox | Assistant to the Growth Pastor

Last week, we looked at 1 Corinthians 13. Verse 2 states: ***"And if I have prophetic powers, and understand all mysteries and all knowledge, and if I have all faith, so as to remove mountains, but have not love, I am nothing."*** Again, in 1 Corinthians 14:1, Paul states: ***"Pursue love, and earnestly desire the spiritual gifts, especially that you may prophesy."*** It must be pretty important for Paul to say it again to the church in Corinth!

Have you ever had to be told something once, then twice, maybe several times? You just did not understand – just did not "get it"? The church in Corinth was struggling with worldly, selfish, immoral behavior. Paul was trying to show them what God desires of them. First, he tells them to pursue love. Pursue it; make it a priority. Love is the greatest gift of the Spirit and the only one that lasts through eternity. All that is done, whether inside the church building, in our homes, in our workplaces, in the grocery store –it is to be done with love. ***"So now faith, hope, and love abide, these three; but the greatest of these is love"*** (1 Corinthians 13:13).

Paul then goes on to talk again about spiritual gifts. They are all given by the Holy Spirit. They are all important. However, the Corinthians were using the gift of tongues improperly, and they felt they were more important than the gift of prophecy. Prophecy can be a foretelling of the future, but is also means to understand scripture, interpret it, and communicate God's message to people in a way they can understand, providing insight, warning, correction, and encouragement. It must be used for building up the church, not for one's personal gain.

The Corinthians were misusing their gifts for selfish gain and needed correction. Have you ever gotten off the "right" path and needed correction? Have you ever been to a psychic, or seen the preacher on the street corner who predicts the end of the world is on such-and-such a date? None of that is biblical. None of that is from a person well versed in scripture, and spoken in love. Many of them are selfish, divisive, only out for personal gain.

In the next few days, Jill will talk about orderly worship, using our spiritual gifts as God intended, in a loving manner for the purpose of edifying the church, not ourselves. Corinth was a church needing these reminders. Maybe we need a reminder too to review our spiritual gifts and to see if we are using them for God's glory.

"HOLY SPIRIT YOU ARE WELCOME HERE"

Donna Fox | Assistant to the Growth Pastor

This is one of my favorite songs. I love the verse that says, ***"You're our living Hope."*** However, what does that really mean? Is He alive? Yes – He's alive in me!
When I accepted Christ as my Lord and Savior as an adult, I had the hardest time understanding the Holy Spirit and His role in this entire thing called salvation. Nobody seemed to talk about Him much. I heard and read lots about God, and about Jesus, but when I read about the Holy Spirit, I was left with lots of questions.

What is His role?
Once I began to understand that when I made the decision to accept Christ, the Holy Spirit began living inside of me, my life was transformed! I began to understand that He lives with us during our time here on earth and teaches us to truly know and follow God.

He is my Counselor, guiding me in my day-to-day decisions. He is my Comforter, with me always and forever, as I am hurting. He convicts me when I am sinning; I call it that "gut feeling" or conscience that gives me that feeling or thought that this just is not right. He is always with me to guide me in the truth. He brings to mind scripture or a sermon I have heard that helps to guide me in my day, or the problem I am facing at the moment. He helps me in my time of prayer. When I just do not know what to say, He intercedes on my behalf.

The Holy Spirit does not just do it all for us, though. We have to do our part. We need to read the Bible, pray, and ask the Holy Spirit to teach us how to live. Look around you on Sunday morning. Do you see the Holy Spirit at work...in you and in others?

WEEK 15

1 Corinthians 14:12

"So with yourselves, since you are eager for manifestations of the Spirit, strive to excel in building up the church."

Paul was seeing strange things happening in the church in Corinth. People were talking in "tongues." It was gibberish. No one understood. No one could interpret. Worship was chaotic. He is saying here that we need to let the Holy Spirit guide us in our worship. He will make our songs, our prayers, and our heart pure to hear what God truly wants us to hear at the time. The chaos in Corinth was not building up the church. However, true worship will edify believers, yourself and others, and they will see in you the manifestation of the Holy Spirit.

Today's prayer: Oh, Holy Spirit, be with me today. Be with me in my decisions, as I hurt, convict me of my sin, and show me the truth.

Holy Spirit, You are welcome here
Come flood this place and fill the atmosphere
Your glory, God, is what our hearts long for
To be overcome by Your presence, Lord
Your presence, Lord

GROW UP!

Donna Fox | Assistant to the Growth Pastor

1 Corinthians 14:20 ***"Brothers, do not be children in your thinking. Be infants in evil, but in your thinking be mature."***

When my grandson was born, it was one of the best days of my life! I became a grandma! He was so precious, making little goo-goo noises and exploring the world around him. He drank only milk. As he grew, he began to learn, to speak, to walk, and to eat solid foods. Now, in first grade, he is learning to read, and to do math. He did not remain as a baby, he grew, and he is maturing. Each day, each month, each year, he grows, learns, and matures. As followers of Christ, so should we. 1 Peter 2:2 says, ***"Like newborn infants, long for the pure spiritual milk, that by it you may grow up into salvation."*** Be thirsty for that pure spiritual milk, crave the Word, read it, soak it in, and let it grow you into maturity.

I accepted Jesus into my life at the age of 33. I was an adult; I could read. I like to think I was mature, at least mature in worldly matters! However, I was a mere babe in my spiritual maturity. I did not know all the Bible stories that my friends grew up with in church. I did not know God's Word as it relates to love, grace, gossip, lying, etc. I was hungry for the Word. I wanted to read every spare minute that I had to learn what truths God had for me to learn.

Merriam-Webster defines maturity as *the quality or state of being mature; especially: full development.* I do not know if we ever fully mature. Even at 90 years old, we are still learning, still gleaning wisdom from what we see, hear, and experience. We are still able to share our knowledge and life lessons (good and bad) with younger generations.

However, we only have a short time here on this earth. Do not use that time to be engaged in unworthy things. Do not give your time and attention to childish and immature matters. Do you spend the majority of your time on Facebook, shopping for fancy clothes, going to movies, working at a job you despise, climbing the corporate ladder? I am not saying those things are wrong; I am saying do not spend your life focused on those things instead of what really matters. In whatever you do, put God first, share the Gospel with others around you, and continue to read the Bible so you can be knowledgeable and become more mature in Godly matters.

Ephesians 4:14-15 says, ***"So that we may no longer be children, tossed to and fro by the waves and carried about by every wind of doctrine, by human cunning, by craftiness in deceitful schemes. Rather, speaking the truth in love, we are to grow up in every way into him who is the head, into Christ."***

DON'T ASK "WHAT CAN MY CHURCH..."

Jill Osmon | Assistant to the Lead Pastors

I was a little intimidated when I found out I would be writing about 1 Corinthians 14; it's a chapter with some topics that can be controversial and create tension within the church. I am not interested in getting into these details, these tensions. What I would love to do is to dig a little deeper and find out why Paul was so passionate about building the church.

Verse 5 of chapter 14 says, ***"Now I want you all to speak in tongues, but even more prophesy. The one who prophesies is greater than the one who speaks in tongues, unless someone interprets, so that the church may be built up."*** The last part of that verse is what stood out to me, ***"...so that the church may be built up."*** Clearly the church was having a pretty epic battle over speaking in tongues, prophesying, among other things and Paul seemed pretty frustrated by it. His whole point is, listen guys, we need to focus on building up the church, let's do that! The Bible speaks of building up the church.

Ephesians 4:16 says, ***"From whom the whole body, joined and held together by every joint with which it is equipped, when each part is working properly, makes the body grow so that it builds itself up in love."***

1 Corinthians 3:10 says, ***"According to the grace of God given to me, like a skilled master builder I laid a foundation, and someone else is building upon it. Let each one take care how he builds upon it."***

In our human capacity, we tend to focus on what we get out of things, not what we can do for others. The Corinthian church was focused on what they were getting out of things, like speaking in tongues, instead of how they could help build up the church. So many times, we fall into that same trap. The church is not a place, or rather, should not be a place, where we come to be attended to, the church should be a place where we come together and do together. That is the heartbeat of our church. We gather with the saints, grow in the Word, and reach the world. We come together to do together, not to be attended to, we cannot be that church; we cannot miss this. Let's build the church together, the church is us, we should be seeking to build and edify so that we can glorify God.

What have you done recently to build the church, not for any personal gain but true building of the church?

YOUR TALENTS

Jill Osmon | Assistant to the Lead Pastors

"What then, brothers? When you come together, each one has a hymn, a lesson, a revelation, a tongue, or an interpretation. Let all things be done for building up." (1 Corinthians 14:26)

What I love about this verse, it implies that when the Corinthian church gathered, they all gave something, when they did reading, sang, or taught, they all participated in being the church. We attend a large church, so I know it can be intimidating, or overwhelming to try to offer your talents to the church. Maybe you do not believe that your talent is usable. Please understand, do not believe that lie from Satan. God honors our abilities and talents when we use them for His glory.

If I could choose one talent, it would be singing. I love to sing, but my love for singing does not match up to my abilities to sing. It does not sound good, trust me, you do not want to be standing next to me when singing; I am that person. I struggled for a long time to know what I could offer the church. I was good at planning. I could not sing, I could not play an instrument, I was not comfortable teaching, working in the nursery was not something anyone wanted me to do, but I could plan and organize. I had no idea how God could use that, but I began to pray, and God continued to give me a passion for events and organization. I fought it for a long time, trying to focus on other things but God kept bringing me back to the ability that He gave me. When I stopped fighting it, He began to use me and the abilities He gave me. No matter what your talent or abilities God had given you (babies, teaching, cleaning, building, hospitality, friendliness, compassion), do not minimize, or ignore it. Find out how God wants you to use those talents and abilities He has given you. Then come together with the church and use them to glorify God and build up His church.

Let's work together and build up the church by bringing our talents and abilities together!

1 CORINTHIANS 14: DEVOTION 6

I CAN SEE CLEARLY NOW

Jill Osmon | Assistant to the Lead Pastors

"For God is not a God of confusion but of peace. As in all the churches of the saints" (1 Corinthians 14:33).

Life can be confusing; it is difficult and emotional, and we can get lost in the immensity of life. We come to points where decisions need to be made, or big life things happen, and we do not understand, we do not know how to navigate them. We get confused.

That confusion can lead to some pretty dark paths, some pretty huge doubts, and we begin to question God. We blame Him for our confusion, for our hurts, and for our lives that do not look like what we want them to. What we have to remember is that God is not in the confusion. ***"For God is not a God of confusion but of peace..."***

How do we get through the confusion? How do we figure out how to calm down and cope? We plant our feet on the truth. Sometimes we think we are, but then another dark time comes, and we are back to questioning everything. See, we cannot simply expect to have peace; we have to pursue it. It will not come naturally to us; we are broken people. However, in Psalms 34:14, God calls us to pursue it... ***"...seek peace and pursue it."*** Do not be passive about having peace, seek it, pursue it, and be intentional.

In Isaiah 54:10 it says, ***"For the mountains be shaken and the hills be removed, but my steadfast love shall not depart from you, and my covenant of peace shall not be removed, says the Lord, who has compassion on you."***

WEEK 15

I love that we have a God that offers peace; we do not have to worry about what the world brings because we have a God that will not keep His peace from us. Though ***"the mountains be shaken... peace shall not be removed."***

16

BACK TO BASICS

Dr. Randy Johnson | Growth Pastor

"Outside of the cross of Jesus Christ, there is no hope in this world. That cross and resurrection at the core of the Gospel is the only hope for humanity. Wherever you go, ask God for wisdom on how to get that Gospel in, even in the toughest situations of life." Ravi Zacharias

The Gospel (death, burial, and resurrection of Jesus Christ) is the core of all of Christianity. Hence, before closing out his letter, Paul brings the Corinthians back to basics.

Now I would remind you, brothers, of the gospel I preached to you, which you received, in which you stand, 2 and by which you are being saved, if you hold fast to the word I preached to you—unless you believed in vain.

How does going back to the Gospel help us refocus in life?

____

____

____

What or where is your identity? ______________________

____

---

3 For I delivered to you as of first importance what I also received: that Christ died for our sins in accordance with the Scriptures, 4 that he was buried, that he was raised on the third day in accordance with the Scriptures, 5 and that he appeared to Cephas, then to the twelve. 6 Then he appeared to more than five hundred brothers at one time, most of whom are still alive, though some have fallen asleep. 7 Then he appeared to James, then to all the apostles. 8 Last of all, as to one untimely born, he appeared also to me. 9 For I am the least of the apostles, unworthy to be called an apostle, because I persecuted the church of God. 10 But by the grace of God I am what I am, and his grace toward me was not in vain. On the contrary, I worked harder than any of them, though it was not I, but the grace of God that is with me. 11 Whether then it was I or they, so we preach and so you believed.

What three events make up the Gospel (verses 3 and 4)?

How many people saw Jesus after the resurrection (verses 5–8)?

How long did Jesus stay on earth after the resurrection (Acts 1:3 says, ***"He presented himself alive to them after his suffering by many proofs, appearing to them during forty days and***

speaking about the kingdom of God.")? ____________________

____

____

How can this help strengthen our faith? ____________________

____

____

12 Now if Christ is proclaimed as raised from the dead, how can some of you say that there is no resurrection of the dead? 13 But if there is no resurrection of the dead, then not even Christ has been raised. 14 And if Christ has not been raised, then our preaching is in vain and your faith is in vain. 15 We are even found to be misrepresenting God, because we testified about God that he raised Christ, whom he did not raise if it is true that the dead are not raised. 16 For if the dead are not raised, not even Christ has been raised. 17 And if Christ has not been raised, your faith is futile and you are still in your sins. 18 Then those also who have fallen asleep in Christ have perished. 19 If in Christ we have hope in this life only, we are of all people most to be pitied.

The Sadducees didn't believe in a resurrection (so they were "sad you see"), but the Pharisees did believe in a resurrection (so they were "fair you see"). The Corinthians were struggling with the topic. What problem is Paul addressing (verse 12)?

____

____

____

What is the big deal if there is no resurrection?

____

____

____

20 But in fact Christ has been raised from the dead, the firstfruits of those who have fallen asleep. 21 For as by a man came death, by a man has come also the resurrection of the dead. 22 For as in Adam all die, so also in Christ shall all be made alive. 23 But each in his own order: Christ the firstfruits, then at his coming those who belong to Christ. 24 Then comes the end, when he delivers the kingdom to God the Father after destroying every rule and every authority and power. 25 For he must reign until he has put all his enemies under his feet. 26 The last enemy to be destroyed is death. 27 For "God has put all things in subjection under his feet." But when it says, "all things are put in subjection," it is plain that he is excepted who put all things in subjection under him. 28 When all things are subjected to him, then the Son himself will also be subjected to him who put all things in subjection under him, that God may be all in all.

What is meant by the phrases by a man came death and in Adam all die? ____

____

____

How is Jesus the antithesis of Adam? ________________

____

____

Who or what is the last enemy to be killed (verse 26)?

____

____

____

What excites you most about Heaven? ________________________

____

____

29 Otherwise, what do people mean by being baptized on behalf of the dead? If the dead are not raised at all, why are people baptized on their behalf? 30 Why are we in danger every hour? 31 I protest, brothers, by my pride in you, which I have in Christ Jesus our Lord, I die every day! 32 What do I gain if, humanly speaking, I fought with beasts at Ephesus? If the dead are not raised, "Let us eat and drink, for tomorrow we die." 33 Do not be deceived: "Bad company ruins good morals." 34 Wake up from your drunken stupor, as is right, and do not go on sinning. For some have no knowledge of God. I say this to your shame.

I die every day – what did it mean to Paul, and what should it mean to us? ____

____

____

Bad company ruins good morals – give examples. Does good company ruin bad morals? ____________________________________

____

____

35 But someone will ask, "How are the dead raised? With what kind of body do they come?" 36 You foolish person! What you sow does not come to life unless it dies. 37 And what you sow is not the body that is to be, but a bare kernel,

perhaps of wheat or of some other grain. 38 But God gives it a body as he has chosen, and to each kind of seed its own body. 39 For not all flesh is the same, but there is one kind for humans, another for animals, another for birds, and another for fish. 40 There are heavenly bodies and earthly bodies, but the glory of the heavenly is of one kind, and the glory of the earthly is of another. 41 There is one glory of the sun, and another glory of the moon, and another glory of the stars; for star differs from star in glory.

What kind of body will we have after the resurrection?

____

____

____

42 So is it with the resurrection of the dead. What is sown is perishable; what is raised is imperishable. 43 It is sown in dishonor; it is raised in glory. It is sown in weakness; it is raised in power. 44 It is sown a natural body; it is raised a spiritual body. If there is a natural body, there is also a spiritual body. 45 Thus it is written, "The first man Adam became a living being"; the last Adam became a life-giving spirit. 46 But it is not the spiritual that is first but the natural, and then the spiritual. 47 The first man was from the earth, a man of dust; the second man is from heaven. 48 As was the man of dust, so also are those who are of the dust, and as is the man of heaven, so also are those who are of heaven. 49 Just as we have borne the image of the man of dust, we shall also bear the image of the man of heaven.

Who is being contrasted here? ________________________

____

____

Why is Paul taking so much time on this topic?

____

____

____

50 I tell you this, brothers: flesh and blood cannot inherit the kingdom of God, nor does the perishable inherit the imperishable. 51 Behold! I tell you a mystery. We shall not all sleep, but we shall all be changed, 52 in a moment, in the twinkling of an eye, at the last trumpet. For the trumpet will sound, and the dead will be raised imperishable, and we shall be changed. 53 For this perishable body must put on the imperishable, and this mortal body must put on immortality. 54 When the perishable puts on the imperishable, and the mortal puts on immortality, then shall come to pass the saying that is written:
"Death is swallowed up in victory."
55 "O death, where is your victory?
O death, where is your sting?"
56 The sting of death is sin, and the power of sin is the law. 57 But thanks be to God, who gives us the victory through our Lord Jesus Christ.

Verse 51 should be on a sign in the church nursery. Actually, what is meant by this verse? ____________________

____

____

Does this passage line up with 1 Thessalonians 4:14-18 (***"For since we believe that Jesus died and rose again, even so, through Jesus, God will bring with him those who have fallen asleep. 15 For this we declare to you by a word from the Lord, that we who are alive, who are left until the***

coming of the Lord, will not precede those who have fallen asleep. 16 For the Lord himself will descend from heaven with a cry of command, with the voice of an archangel, and with the sound of the trumpet of God. And the dead in Christ will rise first. 17 Then we who are alive, who are left, will be caught up together with them in the clouds to meet the Lord in the air, and so we will always be with the Lord. 18 Therefore encourage one another with these words.")?

What is the most comforting thing here as you consider the reality of death? ____

____

____

58 Therefore, my beloved brothers, be steadfast, immovable, always abounding in the work of the Lord, knowing that in the Lord your labor is not in vain.

What are the closing commands Paul gives in this section?

____

____

____

How are we to do these commands? ______________________

____

____

"The best news of the Christian gospel is that the supremely glorious Creator of the universe has acted in Jesus Christ's death and resurrection to remove every obstacle between us and himself so that we may find everlasting joy in seeing and savoring his infinite beauty." John Piper

GO GOSPEL

Noble Baird | Director of Guest Services

The Gospel. I think it is safe to say that there is no greater message ever told or heard other than the Gospel of Christ. As followers of Christ, all we are and all we have is because of the Gospel. Growing up, I attended a private Christian school from kindergarten all the way until I graduated from high school. During that time, I heard the Gospel and the stories of Jesus constantly. However, as I told you a couple of weeks ago, it was not until I was 16 years old and on the streets of Atlanta that I truly heard the Gospel message. It is a time in my life that I will never forget; I can remember it just like it was yesterday.

In 1 Corinthians 15:1-2 Paul writes, ***"Now I would remind you, brothers, of the Gospel I preached to you, which you received, in which you stand, and by which you are being saved."*** Paul sets the tone of this chapter by saying, "Hey, let's take a second, and remember the message of the Gospel. Let's think about what is at the foundation of our faith." I love this. Too often, we are caught up in the business of the church, business of serving, business of the next big event, and we can forget the simple message of the Gospel. We forget that moment when it all clicked and truly became a part of us and not just a message.

"By which you are being saved." What does it mean to truly be saved? Is it simply a prayer that is prayed then we go about our ways of life doing whatever we want? Maybe it is being baptized in a lake that truly sets us apart from the rest, right? Paul tells us the answer right in the passage. The Gospel was preached, received, and now we stand in it. Being a follower of Christ is not like wearing a hat. We cannot simply take it off when we feel like it or throw it on right before we head to church Sunday morning. It is a part of us.

When you stand for something, you not only support it, but you live it. To put it in simple terms, “You can’t talk the talk unless you walk the walk.” So, this week as we begin to take a look into 1 Corinthians 15, I want you to start by remembering when the Gospel message of Christ became real to you. When was that moment when you heard it, received it, and started to truly live it?

TERRIFIC TESTIMONY

Noble Baird | Director of Guest Services

"I did not have a fireworks moment for my salvation. I had a falling in love with Jesus in Sunday school when I was a very young child." I absolutely love this quote from Beth Moore. "A lot of times in the society we live in, bigger is better." Whether it is the more action-packed movie, the most souped up cars, or the most extravagant home whatever it may be, there is always competition for who has the biggest and the best. Sadly, the same has become true of our testimony as followers of Christ. At times, we can begin to idolize those who have the craziest testimony and story of how they came to Christ. Now, know my heart, I love hearing people's testimony. Everyone has his or her own unique story, and it is awesome. However, there does not need to be competition on whose is the best. Just as Beth Moore says, there is nothing wrong with not having a big firework moment.

One of the reasons I love 1 Corinthians 15, is because it is the first recorded account of the resurrection. We know this to be true by the facts that Paul writes within the letter. In 1 Corinthians 15:5-8, Paul records those whom Jesus appeared to after His resurrection. The reason we know this to be the earliest recording of the resurrection is found in 15:6, ***"Then He appeared to more than five hundred brothers at one time, most of whom are still alive, though some have fallen asleep."*** Right here, Paul is declaring the fact that there are over five hundred witnesses alive, during the time that he wrote this letter, whom can attest to the resurrection of Christ. Moreover, it is through this resurrection that our salvation hinges on. Without the resurrection, we have nothing; no testimony, no stories to tell, and no messages to preach.

Those five hundred witnesses were ready and able to give an account of what they had seen. Some of them may have had some crazy stories about what God had done in their lives before they came to believe in Christ and His resurrection. Yet, for others, I bet they simply fell in love with Jesus that morning He appeared to them. As you go throughout your day and this week, remember that every story matters. We are not in a competition; no story is greater or makes someone a better follower of Christ. Just as those five hundred witnesses could attest to the resurrection of Christ, we can also. At the end of the day, we have all fallen in love with an amazing, risen Savior.

GOD IS NOT DEAD

Noble Baird | Director of Guest Services

When I attended Moody Bible Institute, I had the privilege of hearing some amazing speakers and preachers. We always had an annual Founder's Week every February, which celebrated our legacy as a school. Amongst all the speakers that I was able to see and hear over my four years, one that I especially loved hearing was Ravi Zacharias. Zacharias is without a doubt one of the greatest apologists of our time. He has a burning passion for the lost and it is seen in both his writing and speaking. This quote of his, in particular, has really stuck with me, "Outside of the cross of Jesus Christ, there is no hope in this world. That cross and resurrection at the core of the Gospel is the only hope for humanity. Wherever you go, ask God for wisdom on how to get that Gospel in, even in the toughest situations of life."

I love 1 Corinthians 15 because it focuses so much on the resurrection and the Gospel message of Christ. Paul writes in 1 Corinthians 15:13-14, ***"But if there is no resurrection of the dead, then not even Christ has been raised. And if Christ has not been raised, then our preaching is in vain and your faith is in vain."*** Here, Paul is saying it plain and simple; without the resurrection of Christ, we have nothing. The resurrection is the absolute foundation of our faith. It is the resurrection that we preach and the resurrection through which we are saved in Christ.

Zacharias brings up an important point about the resurrection, in that it is the only hope for this world. Everyone in this world is searching for hope. Some find that hope in their job, alcohol, drugs, religion, sex, video games, etc. As followers of Christ, we know the only One, who will bring true hope to all those in this world. So, what does all this mean for us? Urgency. An urgency to spread the Gospel message of Christ. We do not preach in vain, nor is our faith in vain because of the fact that our Savior is not in a grave. Our God is not dead. No, He is very much alive, and He conquered the cross and the grave for every one of us. I do my best to leave you with a personal challenge every day I write and today is no different. With that said, I simply want to reiterate what Zacharias said, "Wherever you go, ask God for wisdom on how to get that Gospel in, even in the toughest situations of life."

1 CORINTHIANS 15: DEVOTION 4

WE HAVE HOPE

Noble Baird | Director of Guest Services

When my grandpa died back in February of 2013, it was a rough time for my family. He would always tell us joke after joke after joke, and I was always amazed at how he remembered not only so many jokes, but also the punch lines for each one! At his funeral, I had the privilege to get up and speak to many of my aunts, uncles, and cousins who I rarely see. For me, speaking at my grandpa's funeral was an opportunity to present the Gospel message of Christ to so much of my family who simply have no relationship with Christ. Truth be told, my parents and I are the only ones from my mother's side of the family who proclaim to be followers of Christ.

Death is never easy; it stinks. As followers of Christ, we have hope. We know that this is not the end, but merely the beginning. In 1 Corinthians 15:52-53 Paul writes, ***"For the trumpet will sound, and the dead will be raised imperishable, and we shall be changed. For this perishable body must put on the imperishable, and this mortal body must put on immortality."*** When Christ returns, those who have passed away before us will be raised. We will no longer have the earthly bodies that can get tired and hurt. Instead, we will receive new heavenly bodies that will last forever.

A month and a half before my grandpa passed away, I went and visited him for the last time in the hospital. I was getting ready to go back to Chicago the next morning, so I stopped at Crittenton Hospital in Rochester. When I got there he was asleep, but the nurse woke him up for me, and he had a big smile when he saw me...I always knew I was his favorite grandchild. He sat up, and we talked about life, school, how the food was, and about how we were going to break him out of the hospital. Just before I left, I asked him if I could pray with him as I always would. He gladly reached out his hand for mine as I prayed with him. After we prayed he looked up at me and told me how proud he was of me, of the man I had become, of my choice to go into full-time ministry, and above all that that he loved me.

I will never forget that amazing day with my grandpa. You see, when my grandpa passed away, I knew I would see him again. I had hope because I knew he had accepted Christ as his personal Lord and Savior. There is no doubt in my mind that one day I will see him again in his new heavenly body, no more hospital stays, no more pain, no more medication, just that big smile and his contagious belly laugh.

In Christ, we have hope. We know that one day we will see our fellow brothers, sisters, and loved ones in Christ again. However, if you take a step back and look at verse 51, Paul tells us how we will all be changed when the trumpet sounds in the twinkle of an eye. We have no idea when Christ will return, but He will. Until that day, we must continue to spread the amazing message of the Gospel to those who are hurting, searching, and without hope. You have that hope, now share it with the world, and make it contagious. I know I want to make it as contagious as my grandpa's smile and his laugh, how about you?

VICTORY

Noble Baird | Director of Guest Services

Victory - something that is chased after by so many in this world. Whether it be a sports game, political race, competition at work, or maybe rolling up the rim on a Tim Horton's coffee cup; whatever it may be people are always trying to win. For my father, he will often remind me of the time he had victory finding an action figure for me for Christmas one year. There was a Star Wars action figure I wanted when I was a child, and my father would constantly check the toy stores for it. He would visit before and after work and make phone calls to toy dealers and comic book stores all over the state. Finally, one morning he arrived at a Toys-R-Us just as they were dropping off the morning shipment and he got his victory!

Now, although that fun victory was about a simple action figure, I want to talk about the greatest victory of all times. In 1 Corinthians 15:54-57 Paul writes of this great victory, ***"When the perishable puts on the imperishable, and the mortal puts on immortality, then shall come to pass the saying that is written: 'Death is swallowed up in victory' 'O death, where is your victory? O death, where is your sting?' The sting of death is sin, and the power of sin is the law. But Thanks be to God, who gives us the victory through our Lord Jesus Christ."*** The greatest victory of all was when Jesus conquered the grave. He defeated death, sin, and hell on the cross when He died for us. He paid the ultimate price, His life, and came out victorious!

I do not know about you, but knowing that through Christ we have won the greatest victory of all, puts all other victories I have had to shame. Nothing can come even close to comparing to the victory we have in Christ. So, I want to encourage you as you go through the rest of this week to remember this victory. Remember the victory we have in Christ and how nothing can take that away from us. I also challenge you not to let this simply be a verse read on paper but to make it a declaration in your life. ***"O death where is your victory? O death where is your sting?"***

1 CORINTHIANS 15: DEVOTION 6

GET BACK UP

Noble Baird | Director of Guest Services

Over this past summer, I became a huge fan of the UFC. Between the immense amount of training, mixed martial arts, and the intensity of the fights themselves, I enjoy watching the sport. Just like any sport, people have their favorite players and in this case, mine is Ronda Rousey. Ronda is simply an incredible fighter. As of March 2016, she was ranked the number 2 female bantamweight fighter in the world. She was formerly the champion until Holly Holm knocked her out in a fight in November 2015. However, if you ask anyone who is a fan of the UFC, they will more than likely agree with the fact that Ronda is one of the absolute best in her field.

As Paul concludes this chapter, he closes by encouraging them to keep up the fight. In 1 Corinthians 15:58 he writes, ***"Therefore, my beloved brothers, be steadfast, immovable, always abounding in the work of the Lord, knowing that in the Lord your labor is not in vain."*** It is not easy being a follower of Christ. In a world that is filled with sin and people who constantly bash the name of Christ, it is tough. Yet, Paul encourages us to be steadfast, immovable, and continually pressing forward for the cause of Christ.

Ronda was knocked down back in November. It was not the first, and I am sure it will not be the last time in her life when she is knocked down. However, one thing she has done repeatedly is get back up. She gets up, gets back to the gym, trains harder, practices longer hours, and presses forward in her sport. She has not given up.

Likewise, as followers of Christ, we must not give up the fight. Yes, we are going to get hurt by this world and even by some of those who are closest to us, but we cannot give up. Just as Paul said, we must be steadfast and immovable in our cause for Christ. This world is going to throw whatever it can at us, to knock us down and take us out of the ring. However, do not let it. Do not let this world and the tools Satan tries to use to take us out to win. Just as we talked about yesterday, Christ has already declared victory for us. I leave you with one final challenge: get in the ring, strap on your gloves, and fight the good fight for Jesus!

17

PS: I STILL LOVE YOU

Dr. Randy Johnson | Growth Pastor

Paul concludes his letter by embracing them as teammates. He encourages them to be involved financially, to welcome Timothy, to recognize Christian service, and to walk strong in love.

Now concerning the collection for the saints: as I directed the churches of Galatia, so you also are to do. 2 On the first day of every week, each of you is to put something aside and store it up, as he may prosper, so that there will be no collecting when I come. 3 And when I arrive, I will send those whom you accredit by letter to carry your gift to Jerusalem. 4 If it seems advisable that I should go also, they will accompany me.

What is significant about the phrase on the first day of every week? ______________________________

____

____

Paul advised the Corinthian church to collect money to support other Christians. How do or should we do this today?

____

____

____

Is there a missionary or ministry you can help financially since you can't help physically? ______________________________

____

____

How should money management enter our relationship with God?

____

____

____

"The Dead Sea is the dead sea because it continually receives and never gives."

5 I will visit you after passing through Macedonia, for I intend to pass through Macedonia, 6 and perhaps I will stay with you or even spend the winter, so that you may help me on my journey, wherever I go. 7 For I do not want to see you now just in passing. I hope to spend some time with you, if the Lord permits. 8 But I will stay in Ephesus until Pentecost, 9 for a wide door for effective work has opened to me, and there are many adversaries.

Paul plans to visit if the Lord permits, what aspects of our calendar need to be more open to God's direction?

In verse nine, Paul points out a wide door for effective work and adversaries. Do these two generally go together? Could the presence of adversaries encourage us?

____

____

"The Christian life is not a constant high. I have my moments of deep discouragement. I have to go to God in prayer with tears in my eyes, and say, 'O God, forgive me,' or 'Help me.'" Billy Graham

10 When Timothy comes, see that you put him at ease among you, for he is doing the work of the Lord, as I am. 11 So let no one despise him. Help him on his way in peace, that he may return to me, for I am expecting him with the brothers.

What description is given of Timothy? ____________________

____

____

How would you want to be described as by your Pastor?

____

____

____

12 Now concerning our brother Apollos, I strongly urged him to visit you with the other brothers, but it was not at all his will to come now. He will come when he has opportunity.

Earlier in this letter, the Corinthians were known as choosing (and causing division) leaders (Paul, Cephas, Apollos). Paul didn't view Apollos as an opponent. Do you have someone in your life that people tend to try to put you at odds with?

____

____

____

13 Be watchful, stand firm in the faith, act like men, be strong. 14 Let all that you do be done in love.

These verses sound very militant. Rewrite these verses in your own words. ____

____

____

Which exhortation do you need to apply in a specific situation in your life right now? ____

____

____

"The bottom line in the Christian life is obedience and most people don't even like the word." Charles Stanley

15 Now I urge you, brothers—you know that the household of Stephanas were the first converts in Achaia, and that they have devoted themselves to the service of the saints—16 be subject to such as these, and to every fellow worker and laborer. 17 I rejoice at the coming of Stephanas and Fortunatus and Achaicus, because they have made up for your absence, 18 for they refreshed my spirit as well as yours. Give recognition to such people.

What should the Corinthians imitate regarding Stephanas and the others? ____

____

____

How should we as Pastors and even the church as a whole give recognition to such people? ____

____

____

19 The churches of Asia send you greetings. Aquila and Prisca, together with the church in their house, send you hearty greetings in the Lord. 20 All the brothers send you greetings. Greet one another with a holy kiss.

How do we apply Greet one another with a holy kiss today?

___

___

___

21 I, Paul, write this greeting with my own hand. 22 If anyone has no love for the Lord, let him be accursed. Our Lord, come! 23 The grace of the Lord Jesus be with you. 24 My love be with you all in Christ Jesus. Amen.

Paul regularly dictated his letters to a scribe. What was he probably hoping to accomplish by saying I, Paul, write this greeting with my own hand? ___

___

___

What is tough love? ___

___

___

What topic have you learned more about or has challenged you most from 1 Corinthians (examples: wisdom, what it means to be spiritual, divisions in the church, church discipline, judging, pride, sexual morality, marriage, rights and freedoms, temptation to sin, the Lord's Supper, gifts of the Spirit, the body of Christ, love, resurrection, giving financially...)? ___

___

___

WEEK 17

"We are all pencils in the hand of a writing God, who is sending love letters to the world." Mother Teresa

1 CORINTHIANS 16: DEVOTION 1

LETTERS TO MY SON: BE WATCHFUL

Pastor Ryan Story | Student Pastor

Above my son's crib, my wife and I put the verses 1 Corinthians 16:13-14: ***"Be watchful, stand firm in the faith, act like men, be strong. Let all that you do be done in love."*** When we were discussing decorating his room, I knew I wanted to put some Scripture on his wall. One day while finishing up reading in 1 Corinthians, I stumbled across the final instructions that Paul was leaving for the church or Corinth. I am not sure why but I felt tasked to teach my son how to live out each one of these. In the same way that Paul wanted the church of Corinth to live for Jesus that is my hope as well.

"The greatest disciples you'll ever develop are not in your church, they are in your home"- Dustin Woodward

Dear Broly,

I made a mistake today. When we were sitting on the couch doing our Monday tradition, watching cartoons, I took my eyes off you for only a moment and somehow you managed to roll off the couch. The moment I heard the thud I knew what had happened, and I felt horrible. I scooped you up, held you until you calmed down and you went back to being your normal crazy self. After that, I put you on the floor and just sat and watched you play. Now I know you are just a baby, but I wish you understood that there are some things that can hurt you. You scare me when you start grabbing electrical cords and putting them in your mouth. I will always be here for you, and I will always be here to watch over you and keep you safe, but soon you will have to keep watch over yourself.

Son, please be watchful of your walk with Jesus. Being able to have a relationship is the biggest blessing that anyone could ask for, but we need to make sure that we are not ruining that relationship. ***"Do you not know that a little leaven leavens the whole lump?"*** (1 Corinthians 5) It seemed like such a small thing to look away from you, and you fell. That is how our walk with God can be. A sin may seem small, quick, and insignificant but please pray to God to help you resist that sin. No sin should ever enter your life without you knowing it. No sin should be able to settle in your heart without being undisturbed.

"There is nothing finer than the point of a needle, but when it has made a hole, it draws all the thread after it" - J.C. Ryle

Broly, Jesus has an amazing plan for you. It may seem like you can let your guard down, or go on a break, but that is what the enemy wants. It took me five seconds to realize that you were on the ground today. When you get older, you will understand that sometimes it can take years to get rid of sin. There are hundreds of barnacles I have on my heart from years of unrepentant sin. I so wish I had been watchful and not let them into my life in the first place. When you fell today, a thought formed. "There are several ways to get down from a high place. Fall or climb down slowly." If you let the little sins grow, you will fall. I hope you learn to ask God to help you when you need someone to watch over you. Keep your eyes open, do not be deceived, and learn how to ask God to help you. Trust me; you will get to watch God do great things if you stay watchful of your life.

LETTERS TO MY SON: STAND FIRM IN THE FAITH

Pastor Ryan Story | Student Pastor

1 Corinthians 16:13-14:
"Be watchful, stand firm in the faith, act like men, be strong. Let all that you do be done in love."

Broly,
I hope you are a sports guy. Right now, your mother is telling me you cannot play hockey or football. I have about 15 years to change her mind, and I hope you can help me. One of my biggest regrets is never playing football in high school. I look at myself and realize that I am a huge guy, and I am pretty sure I was equally as big in high school. I wish I had the courage to play. I think I was afraid of being hit. I played a lot of hockey in my younger days, and I took several checks in my day. Sometimes they hurt sometimes they didn't. The thing I realized was when I was skating and collided with a person it seemed to hurt less than if I was staying still. For some reason, moving forward makes the impact less impactful. That is how life is. If you are not moving forward, if you are not ready to put up any resistance, the world will run you over.

Above your bed, it says, ***"Stand firm in the faith,"*** I want you to stand up for many things, but the one thing I hope you learn to stand for is your faith. Your faith in Jesus is the one thing that brings you strength. Your faith in Jesus is the one thing that gives you purpose. Your faith in Jesus is the one thing that can save you from Hell. When the world is coming at you full speed ahead, let your faith shield you. Let it protect you, because it will. However, this is where I need you to understand that there will be a time where you will have to stand up for your faith in the same way that your faith stands up for you.

It is not popular to live for Jesus. You will lose friends. You will lose opportunities with girls. You will lose out living like a "normal" kid. Also, because you are my son, you will lose out on more because of what God has called me to be. For that, I am sorry, but for that, you are welcome. Son, there will be moments in your walk with Christ where you want to stop fighting. There will be moments when you do not want to push as hard as you can. There will be moments when are ok with letting your guard down. There will be moments that people hate you. There will be moments when people judge you. I beg you to take these words to heart and stand firm in your faith. Jesus stood firm to the point of sweating blood, and all the disciples were martyred. You will have a moment in your life when you will have to stand up for what you believe in. The question for you is, are you going to stand up and take the hit and keep going, or take the hit and fall down and never get up?

1 CORINTHIANS 16: DEVOTION 3

LETTERS TO MY SON: ACT LIKE A MAN

Pastor Ryan Story | Student Pastor

1 Corinthians 16:13-14:
"Be watchful, stand firm in the faith, act like men, be strong. Let all that you do be done in love."

Broly,

Being a man is an interesting thing. Men can watch something on YouTube and become experts at any task; however, true manhood can only be learned by being welcomed into this "fraternity" by another man. Son, since the moment I bit into that cupcake and saw blue, my life changed. You went from being my baby to being my son. As excited as I was, there was also a new feeling I have never felt before. I felt a mixture of excitement and fear with a dash of "over-whelmed-ness." Broly, the hard reality is this; there are not many men in this world. There are tons of adult boys around, but few are men. This world does not need more boys. It needs men! Men that are strong, Godly, and mature. So I challenge you, my son, act like a man.

For years, I feared the day that God would bless me with you. I am terrified of the idea of failing you and not showing you what a man is. I prayed and prayed for weeks when you were first born about how I was going to show you how to be a man, and each time I came to the reality that I will always fall short. I am a failure. I could not figure out how to show you how to be tender and loving and yet be tough as iron. How do I teach you to hold your tongue in meekness and humility, and yet be bold enough to stand up for the things you believe in? How do I teach you to walk with confidence and boldness and be willing to put everyone before yourself? How do I teach a boy to protect his loved ones, and yet turn the other cheek? Sadly, I am horribly unqualified to show you such things, but I knew someone who was.

I realized very quickly that if I am going to show you how to act like a man, I better show you who the perfect man is. True manhood does not mean being perfect; it means trusting in Christ's perfection. Broly, I lived more than half my life without Jesus. I put all of my hopes and dreams in my own hands. I modeled my ways after me. Trust me; a man is not someone who builds his life with his own hands. A true man is someone who allows Jesus to build us into His image. I tried to build my life into what I thought I wanted. I want you to let Jesus build you into the man that you need to become.

The best advice I can give you about growing up is always to have a map. Men do not like maps. Men like to figure out stuff on our own; we like to make our own path. However, without a map, son, we can get lost very quickly. Feeling lost is the worst feeling you could ever experience. Your map is right in front of you. Your map is Jesus. He has always known you. He knows the path you are going to walk. The question is, do you try to read this map? Broly, I cannot make you read the Bible, I cannot make you pray, and I cannot force you to spend quiet time with God. Broly, He is your map. Will you use it?

LETTERS TO MY SON: BE STRONG

Pastor Ryan Story | Student Pastor

1 Corinthians 16:13-14:
"Be watchful, stand firm in the faith, act like men, be strong. Let all that you do be done in love."

Broly,
You are strong. There will never be a moment in your life when I will not tell you this. I hope you always understand what strength is. You are not strong because of what you can lift. You are not strong because you are tough. You are strong because you understand what strength truly is. If you completely give your all physically, you will exhaust yourself time and again. True strength comes when you give yourself completely spiritually.

Life is hard. Life can be unfair. People can be harsh. People will hurt you. There will be times in your life that you will want to give up, but be strong. There is nowhere in the Bible where it says that Jesus is going to make sure that everything will be easy. The truth is Jesus Himself even says, ***"In the world you will have tribulation. But take heart; I have overcome the world"*** (John 16). Your strength does not come from you; it does not come from you grinding harder. Your strength comes from Him. You are strong because of His strength. Your strength comes from surrendering your life to Jesus.

Be strong. Life will be hard. Jesus will help you, but you had better keep moving. A strong man has determination. A strong man never stops moving forward. If life gets hard, keep moving. When you feel like quitting, understand that is not the voice of God. Never quit, refuse to give up because when you embrace the strain of life, you will get His strength. ***"Behold, I have refined***

you, but not as silver; I have tried you in the furnace of affliction" (Isaiah 48). You know I love this verse. Learn to take the pain in order to get the refinement. The strain of life helps build strength. God will use difficult times to make you stronger. If there is never any strain, is there ever any refinement? In times of pain, son, learn to ask God for life, joy, liberty, or/and wisdom. In those moments, He will be there, and He will give you strength.

You will never know how strong God can make you if you are always giving up. Don't look at the pain, don't look at hopelessness, and don't look at the impossible. Broly, grow up and be strong. Grow up realizing that Jesus is your strength. Realize that there is no impossibility with Jesus. Embrace the pain. Embrace the difficulty. Embrace the challenge. Never embrace giving up. Embrace the strength that defeated death, hell, and the grave. Hold tight to Jesus.

Stay strong son. When you keep moving forward, God will open doors that you cannot even imagine.

LETTERS TO MY SON: LET ALL THAT YOU DO BE DONE IN LOVE

Pastor Ryan Story | Student Pastor

1 Corinthians 16:13-14:
"Be watchful, stand firm in the faith, act like men, be strong. Let all that you do be done in love."

Broly,
Read this list.

"Love is patient
Love is kind
Love does not envy or boast;
Love is not arrogant or rude.
Love does not insist on its own way
Love is not irritable or resentful;
Love does not rejoice at wrongdoing, but rejoices with the truth.
Love bears all things, believes all things, hopes all things, endures all things.
Love never ends"

Be all of those things. I hope you took a second to realize how hard that will be.

My last prayer I have for your life is that everything you do in your life is done in love. This will be the hard part. This is hard for me to even challenge you. I cannot look you in the eye and expect you to do these when I can barely handle doing two consistently, but my ceiling will always be your floor and I will do my best to show you how to do it, but I want you to take it further.

Such a small verse holds years of application. When you ride your bike, make sure it is done in love. When you go to school, make sure it is done in love. When you take out the trash, let it be done in love. When you fail, let it be done in love. How in the world does one do that? Also, any act that cannot be done in love should not be done at all, so how does one become better? I could sit here and ask question after question about how one applies this verse to their life, but it would get us nowhere. So let's not look to ourselves to solve this problem, let's look to the one who show us how love is done, Jesus.

"God is love" (1 John 4:8). If you want to become something in this life, look at someone who is a professional. If you want to learn to build, get to know a builder. If you want to learn how to play basketball, go get to know a ball player. If you want to learn how to let every action in your life be love, we need to go to Jesus. I cannot tell you how to do everything, and I cannot write out every way to love. However, I can tell you that if you want to learn how to let every action of your life be done in love, you need to get close to the one who is love. When you get close to Him, it will be amazing to see how these actions will start becoming who you are.

THE OPEN DOOR

Pastor Ryan Story | Student Pastor

Everyone loves the weekends. There is something about knowing that you get to sleep in on Saturday (hopefully) and have two days free of work. I used to love getting up and watching Saturday morning cartoons with a big bowl of cereal. Now for those with kids or housework, I understand the plight that there is no such thing as a weekend. Nonetheless, we all love the weekend. If you are reading this, and went to that dark pessimistic place in your heart and are refusing to come out, try to remember a time when weekends were amazing. Take a second to think about how this weekend will start. Most of us have tasks we need to complete such as yard work, shopping, or simply just spending time with family. When you are making your plan for the day, how often do you think of the opportunity you have every weekend at church?

While Paul was wrapping up his letter to the church in Corinth, he wrote them his "weekend plans." "I will visit you after passing through Macedonia, for I intend to pass through Macedonia, and perhaps I will stay with you or even spend the winter, so that you may help me on my journey, wherever I go. For I do not want to see you now just in passing. I hope to spend some time with you, if the Lord permits. But I will stay in Ephesus until Pentecost, for a wide door for effective work has opened to me, and there are many adversaries" (I Corinthians 16:5-9). As much as Paul wanted to see the people of Corinth, he tells them that he has an amazing opportunity in Ephesus.

In life when we are blessed with any amazing opportunity, we run into adversity. What do you tend to focus on? Many times in life, I know I focus on all the adversity I see rather than the opportunity

I am given. This takes an entire shift in how we view our lives. I wonder if Paul was looking at the advertising in Ephesus, or if he was looking at the opportunity. How did Paul get to this place in life? Paul could have gone to live with the people he knew in Corinth, help that church get some things right, get ready for another journey (which we should all be eager to go on journeys for God), but instead, he stayed in a city that he knew he would run into adversity. He knew he would face people who hated him. Paul did not see the negative, the painful, the awkward, and the struggle in the situation; he saw the opportunity.

Now back to this weekend. What opportunity has God placed in front of you that you have not seized? For many it is getting to church consistently. Let's face it you may have randomly opened your email and saw this devotional. Some of you have the great opportunity to get involved serving. Satan loves to make sure there is always some sort of adversity in the way to keep God's people from serving as Jesus served. Yes, serving takes time, energy, and sometimes-even money. However, are you letting those adversities get in the way of you seeing how God can use you? Now for the coup da grace that most of us struggle with.... inviting someone to church. Inviting someone to church can become present numerous adversities. Those difficulties can range from your own fears and self-consciousness to issues with the person you are trying to invite. No wonder these things pop up, the enemy does not want us, or that person, to get closer to God. So this weekend, take a moment to think of that person whom you know God wants you to bring to church. It can be hard, it can be awkward, but think of the opportunity.

OUR MISSION

Matthew 28:19-20: ***"Go therefore and make disciples of all nations, baptizing them in the name of the Father and of the Son and of the Holy Spirit, teaching them to observe all that I have commanded you. And behold, I am with you always, to the end of the age."***

REACH

At The River Church, you will often hear the phrase, "we don't go to church, we are the Church." We believe that as God's people, our primary purpose and goal is to go out and make disciples of Jesus Christ. We encourage you to reach the world in your local communities.

GATHER

Weekend Gatherings at The River Church are all about Jesus, through singing, giving, serving, baptizing, taking the Lord's Supper, and participating in messages that are all about Jesus and bringing glory to Him. We know that when followers of Christ gather together in unity, it's not only a refresher it's bringing life-change.

GROW

Our Growth Communities are designed to mirror the early church in Acts as having "all things in common." They are smaller collections of believers who spend time together studying the word, knowing and caring for one another relationally, and learning to increase their commitment to Christ by holding one another accountable.

The River Church
8393 E. Holly Rd. Holly, MI 48442
theriverchurch.cc • info@theriverchurch.cc